Current
CONTROVERSIES

The Wage Gap

Other Books in the Current Controversies Series

The Wage Gap

Christina Fisanick, Book Editor

GREENHAVEN PRESS
A part of Gale, Cengage Learning

GALE
CENGAGE Learning™

Detroit • New York • San Francisco • New Haven, Conn • Waterville, Maine • London

Christine Nasso, *Publisher*
Elizabeth Des Chenes, *Managing Editor*

© 2008 Greenhaven Press, a part of Gale, Cengage Learning

Gale and Greenhaven Press are registered trademarks used herein under license.

For more information, contact:
Greenhaven Press
27500 Drake Rd.
Farmington Hills, MI 48331-3535
Or you can visit our Internet site at gale.cengage.com

ALL RIGHTS RESERVED.
No part of this work covered by the copyright herein may be reproduced, transmitted, stored, or used in any form or by any means graphic, electronic, or mechanical, including but not limited to photocopying, recording, scanning, digitizing, taping, Web distribution, information networks, or information storage and retrieval systems, except as permitted under Section 107 or 108 of the 1976 United States Copyright Act, without the prior written permission of the publisher.

For product information and technology assistance, contact us at

Gale Customer Support, 1-800-877-4253
For permission to use material from this text or product, submit all requests online at www.cengage.com/permissions

Further permissions questions can be emailed to permissionrequest@cengage.com

Articles in Greenhaven Press anthologies are often edited for length to meet page requirements. In addition, original titles of these works are changed to clearly present the main thesis and to explicitly indicate the author's opinion. Every effort is made to ensure that Greenhaven Press accurately reflects the original intent of the authors. Every effort has been made to trace the owners of copyrighted material.

Cover image copyright Valentin Mosichev, 2008. Used under license of Shutterstock.com.

LIBRARY OF CONGRESS CATALOGING-IN-PUBLICATION DATA

The wage gap / Christina Fisanick, book editor.
    p. cm. -- (Current controversies)
  Includes bibliographical references and index.
  ISBN-13: 978-0-7377-3968-8 (hardcover)
  ISBN-13: 978-0-7377-3969-5 (pbk.)
  1. Wages--United States--Juvenile literature. 2. Pay equity--United States--Juvenile literature. 3. Wages--Women--United States--Juvenile literature. 4. Minorities--Employment--United States--Juvenile literature. 5. Wages--Effect of education on--United States--Juvenile literature. I. Fisanick, Christina.
  HD4975.W29 2008
  331.2'1530973--dc22
                                            2008007483

Printed in the United States of America
1 2 3 4 5 6 7 12 11 10 09 08

Contents

Chapter 1: Is the Wage Gap Between Men and Women Narrowing?

Yes: The Wage Gap Between Men and Women Is Narrowing

Chapter 3: Is the Wage Gap Between the Races Due to Discrimination?

Chapter 4: Is Education Key to Reducing Wage Gaps?

Foreword

By definition, controversies are "discussions of questions in which opposing opinions clash" (Webster's Twentieth Century Dictionary Unabridged). Few would deny that controversies are a pervasive part of the human condition and exist on virtually every level of human enterprise. Controversies transpire between individuals and among groups, within nations and between nations. Controversies supply the grist necessary for progress by providing challenges and challengers to the status quo. They also create atmospheres where strife and warfare can flourish. A world without controversies would be a peaceful world; but it also would be, by and large, static and prosaic.

The Series' Purpose

The purpose of the *Current Controversies* series is to explore many of the social, political, and economic controversies dominating the national and international scenes today. Titles selected for inclusion in the series are highly focused and specific. For example, from the larger category of criminal justice, *Current Controversies* deals with specific topics such as police brutality, gun control, white collar crime, and others. The debates in *Current Controversies* also are presented in a useful, timeless fashion. Articles and book excerpts included in each title are selected if they contribute valuable, long-range ideas to the overall debate. And wherever possible, current information is enhanced with historical documents and other relevant materials. Thus, while individual titles are current in focus, every effort is made to ensure that they will not become quickly outdated. Books in the *Current Controversies* series will remain important resources for librarians, teachers, and students for many years.

In addition to keeping the titles focused and specific, great care is taken in the editorial format of each book in the series. Book introductions and chapter prefaces are offered to provide background material for readers. Chapters are organized around several key questions that are answered with diverse opinions representing all points on the political spectrum. Materials in each chapter include opinions in which authors clearly disagree as well as alternative opinions in which authors may agree on a broader issue but disagree on the possible solutions. In this way, the content of each volume in *Current Controversies* mirrors the mosaic of opinions encountered in society. Readers will quickly realize that there are many viable answers to these complex issues. By questioning each author's conclusions, students and casual readers can begin to develop the critical thinking skills so important to evaluating opinionated material.

Current Controversies is also ideal for controlled research. Each anthology in the series is composed of primary sources taken from a wide gamut of informational categories including periodicals, newspapers, books, U.S. and foreign government documents, and the publications of private and public organizations. Readers will find factual support for reports, debates, and research papers covering all areas of important issues. In addition, an annotated table of contents, an index, a book and periodical bibliography, and a list of organizations to contact are included in each book to expedite further research.

Perhaps more than ever before in history, people are confronted with diverse and contradictory information. During the Persian Gulf War, for example, the public was not only treated to minute-to-minute coverage of the war, it was also inundated with critiques of the coverage and countless analyses of the factors motivating U.S. involvement. Being able to sort through the plethora of opinions accompanying today's major issues, and to draw one's own conclusions, can be a complicated and frustrating struggle. It is the editors' hope that *Current Controversies* will help readers with this struggle.

Introduction

In 1968, Lilly Ledbetter began working in a Goodyear Tire plant as a supervisor. Twenty years later she received an anonymous note that brought to her attention that she was being paid substantially less than her male coworkers. Within a month of receiving the note, Ledbetter filed discrimination charges with the Equal Employment Opportunity Commission (EEOC), which enforces federal laws that prohibit job discrimination. Ledbetter's case went to the Supreme Court, and it was ruled that she filed her complaint too late. According to the Supreme Court's ruling, Ledbetter should have filed her complaint within 180 days of receiving her first discriminatory paycheck. If it had not been for the statute of limitations period, Ledbetter would have been protected under Title VII of the Civil Rights Act of 1964 since it prohibits discrimination based on race, color, religion, sex, and national origin. In June 2007, Representative George Miller (D-CA) and other top House Democrats introduced the Lilly Ledbetter Fair Pay Act. If the act is passed, each paycheck will be considered a separate discriminatory act if the paycheck is less than it otherwise would have been due to the employee's race, color, religion, sex, and national origin.

Supporters of the Lilly Ledbetter Fair Pay Act believe it is unrealistic to expect workers to know that they are victims of wage discrimination within 180 days of the first occurrence, especially given that most workers do not discuss their paychecks with their colleagues, which makes it extremely difficult for employees to know if they have been the victims of pay discrimination. Congressman Joe Sestak has stated, "To put an arbitrary limit on when employees can file charges regarding discrimination places an unfair burden on the employees who may not be aware of their rights. This is an easy thing for us to fix and we need to do that now."

Opponents of the bill argue that it is unfair to businesses because it eliminates time requirements for filing compensation discrimination claims and waives the statute of limitations for claims involving pensions, vacation benefits, and all other compensation. They believe the act will force employers to defend past employment decisions, allow plaintiffs to file lawsuits based on circumstantial evidence, delay employees' filing of discrimination complaints, create excessive litigation, and include the "pension annuity check rules," which would allow employees to bring charges against an employer as long as they are receiving retirement benefits. Jason Straczewski, director of employment and labor policy for the National Association of Manufacturers, has stated, "Essentially, this legislation would open the door to lawsuits that employers cannot defend."

It remains to be seen whether the Lilly Ledbetter Fair Pay Act will become law, but disagreements about its ramifications are sure to continue. The failure of organizations to address wage discrimination invites such proposed government regulation. In addition to wage disparities between the sexes, the viewpoints in *Current Controversies: The Wage Gap* examine such discrepancies among employees from different races, economic backgrounds, and educational levels.

CHAPTER 1

Is the Wage Gap Between Men and Women Narrowing?

Chapter Preface

"We know the enormous economic impact the wage gap has on the lives of working women—less money in the paycheck, less money for retirement, less money to invest, less money to plain live on," Patricia E. Cornish stated at a May 2007 Business and Professional Women's club meeting. The U.S. Department of Labor defines the glass ceiling as "those artificial barriers based on attitudinal or organizational bias that prevent qualified individuals from advancing upward in their organization into management-level positions." The glass ceiling is often blamed for the wage gap between men and women. People who believe a glass ceiling exists blame it for the inability of women to earn promotions and raises. Others believe the glass ceiling does not exist and argue that there are other, more concrete reasons why women do not earn promotions and raises as frequently as men.

People who argue glass ceilings exist in today's workplace point out that women are routinely passed up for raises and promotions, preventing them from earning equal pay. A study conducted by the National Association for Female Executives found a gap in the salaries of men and women with identical jobs and experience, even in professions dominated by women, such as teaching, nursing, and public relations. In addition, a study conducted by Catalyst, an organization that studies women in the workplace, found that women who display feminine traits are regarded as less competent among their colleagues. However, if a woman displays "macho" behavior they are thought of as harsh. The Catalyst study also revealed that female executives who wear sexy clothes at work are thought to be less competent, while females who hold traditionally female positions and wear sexy clothes at work are not considered to be less competent. Such stereotypes regarding women in the workplace contribute to the male-female wage gap, those who a glass ceiling exists maintain.

Others argue that a glass ceiling does not exist in today's workplace. They believe factors other than sex discrimination contribute to the male-female wage gap. The responsibilities that women have at home are thought to be one of the biggest contributors to this gap. After all, women are more likely than men to take time off from work to care for their children and to handle household responsibilities. In *It's Not a Glass Ceiling, It's a Sticky Floor*, author Rebecca Shambaugh suggests that women need to stop blaming men and the glass ceiling and start establishing competence, taking credit for accomplishments, negotiating, and networking. Shambaugh asserts that women inadvertently sabotage their own careers. According to Shambaugh, "Women are more likely than men to shy away from leadership roles, to get bogged down in perfectionism, and to avoid career-boosting changes out of a misplaced sense of loyalty." In addition to these factors, the failure of women to negotiate their starting wages is thought to be one of the leading causes of the male-female wage gap since raises are often based on a percentage of current pay. In a study conducted by Carnegie Mellon University economics professor Linda Babcock, only 12 percent of women negotiated their salary while 52 percent of men negotiated their salary. Regardless of sex, those who negotiate their salary are paid 7–8 percent more than those who do not negotiate.

Since many women today expect to have successful careers and also need to be financially independent, understanding whether or not a glass ceiling exists in the workplace can help women reach their professional, financial, and personal goals, many argue. The viewpoints in the following chapter explore whether or not the male-female wage gap is narrowing in today's workplace.

The Wage Gap Between Men and Women Is Narrowing

Marc Doms and Ethan Lewis

Marc Doms is a senior economist employed by the Federal Reserve Bank of San Francisco. Ethan Lewis is an assistant economics professor at Dartmouth University.

A ccording to several measures, the difference in wages between men and women, the so-called "male-female wage gap" (MFWG), has shrunk substantially—by about half—over the past several decades. This phenomenon has been the subject of much research, speculation, and contention. For example, some seek to explain why the gap narrowed so dramatically in the 1980s only to narrow much more slowly in subsequent years. Others have considered the role of new technology, which may have helped level the playing field between the sexes; this view recalls the rise of office work at the turn of the 20th century, which is also thought to have benefited women.

In this [viewpoint], we focus on an important portion of the research in this area, particularly as it pertains to the very sharp decline in the MFWG during the 1980s. We summarize three of the more well-known possible explanations: declining discrimination against women, rising skills and workforce attachment of women, and changing selection. While each has strong merit in its own right, none has come to be the dominant explanation. We speculate that it may be fruitful, though challenging, to consider whether these three explanations worked together, occurring simultaneously and reinforcing one another, to result in the sharp narrowing of the MFWG in the 1980s.

Mark Doms and Ethan Lewis, "The Narrowing of the Male-Female Wage Gap," reprinted from Federal Reserve Bank of San Francisco's Economic Letter 2007-17 (June 29, 2007). The opinions expressed in this article do not necessarily reflect the views of the management of the Federal Reserve Bank of San Francisco, or of the Board of Governors of the Federal Reserve System.

Measuring the Male-Female Wage Gap

There are several ways to compare the wages of males and females, and no single measure is perfect or preferable in every instance. The method most often used in academic studies is to examine hourly wages for only full-time workers using data sets such as the Current Population Survey (CPS) or Decennial Census. These studies typically measure the difference in wages between the sexes after controlling for differences in years of education and age. This approach ensures that, for example, the wage of a 50-year-old female with a post-college degree is not directly compared to that of an 18-year-old male who dropped out of high school. . . .

Decline in Discrimination

Differences in pay between men and women may be partly the result of discrimination against women in the workplace. Such gender discrimination may have lessened, especially as a result of changes that occurred in the 1970s and 1980s. For example, in *Pittsburgh Press Co. v. Pittsburgh Commission on Human Relations* (1973), the U.S. Supreme Court upheld an ordinance that prohibited publishing job advertisements that sorted positions into "Help Wanted: Male" and "Help Wanted: Female." In addition, [American University professor Rita J. Simon and Eastern University assistant professor Jean M. Landis] found that opinion polls showed that men's willingness to accept women in the workplace rose considerably in the 1970s and 1980s.

Unfortunately, ascertaining whether the MFWG has shrunk because of lessening discrimination against women is difficult, because measuring discrimination itself, let alone changes in discrimination, is difficult.

Rising Skills and Workforce Attachment

Unlike discrimination, trends in the skills of women and their attachment to the workforce (that is, their staying in the workforce) since the 1970s are more easily demonstrable. In terms of education, [Harvard professors Claudia Goldin and Lawrence F. Katz and Princeton professor Ilyana Kuziemko have determined that] American women born after 1960 began completing college at higher rates than men. Perhaps more importantly, during the 1970s, women entered professional graduate programs and went on to professional careers in record numbers. This is important because professional occupations tend to have higher pay than many of the jobs that used to be listed in the "Help Wanted: Female" ads. Additionally, women's attachment to the labor force may have increased. For instance, opinion surveys show a dramatic rise in the proportion of women who say they planned to work at age 35 during the 1970s. Also, . . . from 1983 to 2006, the median job tenure rose noticeably for women but remained relatively unchanged for men.

Rising wages and work experience of women could account for some of the increase in women's relative wages in the 1980s and 1990s.

These trends could help reduce the measured MFWG in several ways. An increased attachment of women to their careers would tend to raise women's average wages by lengthening their average work experience. If, for a given age and education, women gained more experience, then their wages relative to men's would be expected to increase. Similarly, if women made career investments that are not picked up in surveys (such as what they study in school instead of years of schooling), then that could lead to a narrowing in the measured MFWG.

Establishing the relative importance of the rise in workplace human capital among women on the narrowing of the MFWG, however, has not been straightforward. One reason is that the data sets used most frequently in such analyses contain only indirect measures of either workplace experience or career investments. For example, potential work experience in many studies is derived using the age and education of workers in the sample. By contrast, [Francine D. Blau, Cornell University professor of industrial and labor relations and labor economics, and Lawrence M. Kahn, Cornell professor of labor economics and collective bargaining,] use a data set that does contain years of actual work experience. They found that the rising wages and work experience of women could account for some of the increase in women's relative wages in the 1980s and 1990s. They also found that human capital (a combination of work experience and education) of women increased in the 1980s at about the same pace as it did in the 1990s. So although the increase in human capital may have helped close the MFWG, the human capital story says little about why the MFWG closed faster in the 1980s than it did in the 1990s.

Changing Selection

As stated earlier, the MFWG is usually computed using only full-time workers. However, full-time workers may not be representative of the population. Put another way, not everybody works, and economists believe that people's decisions to work or not depend, in part, on what they *would* earn if they did work, their so-called "earnings potential." Therefore, researchers have studied how much the decline in the MFWG may reflect the selective entry of women with high earnings potential into working. [Casey Mulligan, University of Chicago economics professor, and Yona Rubinstein, Brown University economics professor,] argue that the "stay-at-home" women of the 1960s had high earnings potential compared to those who were working; in other words, they were disproportionately women who would have had high pay if they had chosen to have a career. During the 1970s and 1980s the pay for high-skill and professional jobs increased relative to the pay for low-skill jobs. This better pay may have induced women with high earnings potential to pursue careers rather than stay at home. This latter point is buttressed by [Sandra E. Black, assistant economics professor at UCLA, and Chinhui Juhn, University of Houston economics professor].

Since changes in women's earnings potential cannot be observed directly (one only observes the wages of those who are actually working), Mulligan and Rubinstein offer indirect evidence to support their story. They show that two groups of women likely to have high earnings potential—women with high "IQs" and women with educated mothers—have increased their propensity to work significantly more than other women. In addition, they show that wages grew more quickly over the past 30 years for the kinds of women who were least likely to work in the 1960s—for example, married women with children—and less quickly for women who always had higher rates of participation, such as single women. Overall, Mulligan and Rubinstein suggest that most of the closing of the MFWG was due to changing selection.

While many might agree that changing selection played a role in the increase in women's wages—due in part to Mulligan and Rubinstein's evidence—there is less consensus over how much changing selection contributed to the increase in women's pay. For instance, Blau and Kahn, using other methods, suggest that the impact is much smaller.

Possible Interactions

Exploring whether and how these three explanations may have worked together to narrow the MFWG so dramatically in the 1980s is challenging both theoretically and empirically, and it is beyond the scope of this [viewpoint]. However, we believe it may be a fruitful avenue to pursue. For example, consider the link between the decline in discrimination and rising skills among women: It is conceivable that less discrimination reinforced women's decisions to invest more in their own human capital, perhaps by furthering their education or pursuing more lucrative occupational paths. The decline in discrimination also could be linked to the selection explanation, in that it may have lured women with high earnings potential into the labor market. The causality between discrimination and labor force attachment could also go the other direction: For example, greater attachment to the labor force may itself help reduce discrimination if the perceptions of women's attachment to the labor force change as a consequence. Clearly, the phenomenon of the MFWG remains a rich field of research, not only to understand the rapid narrowing of the gap in the 1980s and the slower narrowing in later years but also the persistence of the gap today.

Women Are Taking Action to Narrow the Wage Gap

Dawn Klingensmith

Dawn Klingensmith is a University of Pittsburgh School of Business graduate employed at Ernst & Young, business consulting firm.

In the three decades since women blazed trails into corporate America, the path has become increasingly easier.

Yet there's a hitch: Far short of the executive suite, the trail peters out.

The expanse between middle management and the upper echelon marks "the next frontier" for women in business, said Deborah Merrill-Sands, dean of the Simmons School of Management in Boston.

A mere 1.2 percent of CEOs [chief executive officers] of Fortune 500 companies in 2004 were women, according to Catalyst, a New York–based organization that studies workplace gender issues. And women made up just 16 percent of corporate officers.

In the next 10 years or so, we'll see a significant rise in the number of women in top leadership positions.

Research disproves the oft-cited explanations that women abandon careers to raise kids and that they crave power less than men do, Merrill-Sands said. Persisting gender biases are largely to blame for the dearth of female corporate officers, she said. Simmons surveys of 1,000 professional and managerial women found that nearly half aspire to the highest leadership positions in their organizations.

If you're striving, too, take heart: Women's prospects look promising, Merrill-Sands said.

Getting to the Top

"If we look back over the last 30 years, we've seen some significant advancements," she said, adding that the percentage of middle managers who are women has risen to 50 from 4 in the 1970s. "In the next 10 years or so, we'll see a significant rise in the number of women in top leadership positions."

Unfortunately, there's no map to the top. Women who already have forged ahead can give pointers but no sure-fire plan for success.

"People can offer advice, but the reality is, we all have to map out our own path," said Diane Aigotti, treasurer of Chicago's Aon Corp.

Proper preparation can make for a swifter, smoother journey, though. Here are some practical tips and insights female executives from around Chicago shared with WN on navigating the corporate roadways:

If your final destination is the CEO suite, you definitely should:

Gain plenty of profit-and-loss [P&L] experience. Men still hold 90 percent of the P&L positions at the nation's largest corporations, according to the National Association for Female Executives. "Those are the jobs that provide essential bottom-line experience for boardroom and CEO slots," President Betty Spence said.

In fact, P&L experience is practically a prerequisite. How do you snag these plum positions? You ask for them.

But if the cat's got your tongue:

Read *Women Don't Ask: Negotiation and the Gender Divide.* by Linda Babcock and Sara Laschever. As this book shows, "Women negotiate very effectively on behalf of their companies, but not on their own behalf," said Victoria Medvec, executive director of the Center for Executive Women at Northwestern University's Kellogg School of Management.

Their failure in this regard helps explain the persisting salary gap between men and women and also undermines their efforts to advance. "A common mistake women make is not asking for the tools they need to be successful, like staff increases and other resources," Medvec said.

Communicate your value to the organization. . . . Talk about your accomplishments and make sure key people in the right places are aware of them.

Women also mistakenly believe that raises and promotions come automatically on a silver platter to hard workers, Aigotti said. You need to ask for what you want, and be specific, she advised: "Capitalism is competitive. Have some chutzpah. If you don't ask, someone else will."

Communicate

To outshine other askers, it helps to:

Communicate your value to the organization. "It's important to talk about your accomplishments and make sure key people in the right places are aware of them," Merrill-Sands said. Emphasize the connection between these accomplishments and your organization's bottom line or goals and objectives.

When New York–based Deloitte, a leading provider of audit, tax, consulting and financial-advisory services, asked Ellen Gabriel to lead a companywide initiative to retain and advance women, she worried that her work on the project would be undervalued despite its apparent importance. She put together an analysis showing that as a result of her efforts, the company was able to reduce attrition of women by a certain percentage, which annually saved millions of dollars, Merrill-Sands said.

Gabriel subsequently was elected to the company's board of directors. (She died in 1999 of breast cancer, and the Deloitte Ellen Gabriel Professorship for Women and Leadership was established in honor of her achievements at the Simmons School of Management.)

Touting your achievements might be easier if you:

Create a portfolio documenting your successes. Warm fuzzies, not just facts and figures, should have a place in this brag book.

"You should include e-mails of congratulations from senior management and colleagues, articles you published, awards you won, and anything else that makes you proud," said Chicago entrepreneur Alison Chung, a former law-firm chief information officer whose 8-year-old firm, TeamWerks, specializes in computer forensics. "On a bad day, when no one pats you on the back, you can look at it and smile and pat yourself on the back."

You should also peruse the portfolio before annual performance evaluations to boost your confidence, she added.

Mentors

Back pats are great, but for candid feedback, you should:

Find a mentor. Ask whether your company takes part in Menttium 100, a yearlong program that matches high-potential female nominees with male or female mentors in a complementary field, advised Lisa Tegtmeyer, director of operations at CDW Corp. in Vernon Hills.

Single out an outstanding individual who can give you some pointers.

Spence said mentor seekers should play the field. "People I speak with say they have three times the amount of work they used to have," she said. "Everyone's overloaded."

Trying to initiate an ongoing, one-on-one mentoring relationship with a stressed superior might not be the most productive tack. Instead, select several "simultaneous" or "serial" mentors (more like tutors) for specific short-term assistance, Spence recommended. Start by honestly evaluating your skill set to determine which areas need work. Weak on making presentations? Single out an outstanding individual who can give you some pointers.

A mentor might boost you as high as the glass ceiling. In order to break through, though, you'll likely need to:

Find a sponsor. Medvec said corporate decision-makers "unconsciously think of leaders as men," so you'll need a sponsor—a high-ranking, influential person within your organization—to advocate for your advancement. Special task forces are one way to gain access to sponsors.

When leadership positions become available, a sponsor will "put your name on the table and make a clear argument why you should be considered," Medvec said.

It's your responsibility to get convincing data into this person's hands, she added.

Hire Responsibly

Your curriculum vitae will more likely be convincing if you:

Surround yourself with a super team. "As soon as you're in a position to hire people, it's critical to take the time to find really great employees," said Martha Dustin Boudos, chief financial officer of Morningstar Inc., a Chicago-based mutual fund and stock research company. "Your success depends on it."

Don't hire too hastily. "People get desperate when there's a hole in their staff and tend to think that having someone is better than having no one, but actually the opposite is true: It's always better to have no one than the wrong person in a job," Boudos said.

Once you've assembled a solid team, make sure its success reflects back on you. Always give credit where credit is due, but "at some point you have to associate your team's success with your leadership, your involvement," Boudos said.

The right wording will call attention to your contributions without claiming too much credit, Merrill-Sands said. When reporting to supervisors or the board of directors, "Don't say, 'We're very proud that we've accomplished X, Y and Z.'" Instead, she advised, "Say, 'I'm very proud that I and my team have accomplished these things.'"

External Auditors

They say it's lonely at the top, but not if you:

Find one or more external advisers. The higher you advance in your organization, the more you'll find that folks around you "have their own agendas," Merrill-Sands said. So you may need to look elsewhere for objective advice.

Merrill-Sands' colleague, Saj-nicole Joni, wrote *The Third Opinion: How Successful Leaders Use Outside Insight to Create Superior Results* to underscore the importance of soliciting such input. Joni's research found that CEOs who had one or more external advisers were more objective; made sounder decisions; developed a broader and deeper understanding of their industries; and were ultimately more successful.

Serving on not-for-profit boards is one way to meet prospective advisers, Merrill-Sands said. "And since you'll be working side-by-side, you can develop a relationship with them while getting a sense of their strengths and weaknesses."

Ditch Plans and Explore Possibilities

Studying economics and political science as an undergraduate, Diane Aigotti had no idea how she would use her degrees. "My only goal at the time was to find work that was challenging and meaningful," said Aigotti, treasurer of the Chicago-based insurance broker Aon Corp.

She went on to earn an MBA at the University of Notre Dame and afterward did a series of internships. "But nothing really inspired me," she said.

With no set career plan, Aigotti cold-called the City of Chicago and landed an entry-level job as a budget analyst. She intended to stay for a short time while figuring out what she wanted to do. Within 3 ½ years, though, she had risen through the ranks to become the city's budget director.

The public sector typically doesn't pay as well as the private sector, so to attract and retain good workers, public-sector employers advance young people more rapidly to positions of power, said Aigotti, who went on to work for University of Chicago Hospitals for two years before joining Aon in 2000.

Recognize and take advantage of opportunities that come along unexpectedly.

Whenever young people ask Aigotti for career guidance, she gives them the same advice: "Don't feel like you need to map out a path and stick to that path throughout your career. As my own experience shows, some of the best opportunities come in ways you wouldn't have anticipated."

The problem is, most young people don't want to hear it. "What I often find with young people is that they'll ask for advice, but what they really want is a mapped-out path," she said. "There's no defined recipe for success. The only thing that seems to hold true from one success story to another is the ability to recognize and take advantage of opportunities that come along unexpectedly."

San Francisco author Robin Wolaner said she, too, has found that most young people "earnestly believe that they need a plan for their progression through jobs and life."

The reason? "People used to have kids; now, they parent, which involves dragging their kids from one planned activity after another," said Wolaner, a former media executive whose book, *Naked in the Boardroom: A CEO Bares Her Secrets So You Can Transform Your Career*, includes the chapter "Burn Your Career Plan."

"Everything is organized and structured as opposed to sending the kids outside with a ball to amuse themselves," she said.

Yasmin Bates, an executive vice president of Harris Trust and Savings Bank in Chicago, said college students now are expected to gain internship experience, so many start specializing before graduation. In contrast, when Bates went to work for Harris 29 years ago after graduating from the University of Illinois at Urbana-Champaign, the company enrolled her in a general management program to learn various aspects of the business. "It was OK that I didn't know exactly what I wanted to do," she said.

By mistaking exploration for aimlessness, young people might be limiting their possibilities, said Aigotti, who, at 40, still ponders what she wants to be when she "grows up."

"If you asked me where I wanted to be five years from now, I honestly couldn't tell you," she said. "It's not as if I don't have goals, but I'm not like some people who know for certain that they want to be in this position at a company of this or that size making X amount of money. Half the fun in life is the unexpected. If everything's planned, what's the fun of that?"

Women's Wages Have Increased More than Men's

Jessica Nelson

Jessica Nelson is an employment economist with the Oregon Employment Department and has written extensively about employment issues.

Over the past several decades, women have increased their participation in the labor force. They are more heavily represented in some industries in the economy, while other industries continue to work to recruit them. As women have joined the labor force in greater numbers, their wages have improved compared with those of men, but a gap remains.

Women in the Labor Force

In 1970, 43.3 percent of women age 16 or older in the United States were part of the labor force. The rate grew continually for about three decades before reaching what appears to be a peak labor force participation rate for women of 60.0 percent in 1999. Since 1999, the rate has held between 59 and 60 percent, coming in at 59.3 percent in 2005. It is unclear whether the decades-long increase in women's labor force participation rate has ended.

Those decades did help to close the gap between the labor force participation of men and women. In 1970, men in the United States had a labor force participation rate of 79.7 percent. Over thirty-plus years, that rate drifted slowly down to 73.3 percent in 2005.

Labor force participation rates by gender in Oregon are quite similar to national rates. In Oregon in 2005, an estimated 59.0 percent of women were in the labor force, compared with 73.3 percent of men.

Jessica Nelson, "Working Women: Participation and the Earnings Gap," Oregon Employment Department, January 23, 2007. www.qualityinfo.org.

Women's Work Today

Estimates from the U.S. Census Bureau's American Community Survey for 2005 show the percentage of Oregon women employed in each major industry, as well as the percentage of industry employment made up by women. Women account for an estimated 38.0 percent of full-time year-round workers in Oregon, compared with a 40.6 percent share in the United States.

More women work in educational services, health care and social assistance (27.3%) than in any other industry group. Many women also work in retail trade (12.5%), finance, insurance, real estate, rental and leasing (11.3%), and manufacturing (10.9%).

As a share of industry employment, there are only two industries where women are estimated to make up more than half of full-time year-round workers. In educational services, health care and social assistance 68.4 percent of workers are women. Finance, insurance, real estate, rental and leasing employment is 56.3 percent female.

As women have joined the labor force in greater numbers, diversified their industry participation, and increased their education levels, pay gaps have diminished.

Construction has the lowest representation of women working full-time year-round, at only 7.3 percent of the construction workforce. Agriculture, forestry, fishing, hunting, and mining also have a small share of women at 18.4 percent of the workforce. Though one out of 10 working Oregon women is in manufacturing, they represent less than a quarter (23.7%) of the industry's workforce.

Wage Disparities Decreasing

Pay equity has been a gender equality issue, taken up by the women's rights movement, for decades. As women have joined the labor force in greater numbers, diversified their industry participation, and increased their education levels, pay gaps have diminished, but a gap continues to exist in the pay of female and male workers in the economy today.

Median weekly earnings of full-time female workers in the United States were $182 in 1979, compared with $292 for men. This put women's earnings at 62.3 percent of men's earnings. In 2005, women's median weekly earnings were $585, and men's were $722, putting women's earnings at 81.0 percent of men's earnings. Between 1979 and 2005, women's earnings increased 221 percent, while men's earnings increased 147 percent.

Accounting for the education level of female and male workers does not remove the disparity. At all levels of education, women have lower median weekly earnings than men. The earnings gap is largest for workers with a professional degree. In that category, women's weekly earnings are $1,128 and men's are $1,554, meaning that women's earnings are still only 72.6 percent of men's for people with professional degrees.

Educational attainment is very similar between the genders up through the bachelor degree level; it is only in professional and doctorate degrees that women lag behind, with 2.1 percent of women in Oregon possessing these degrees compared to 4.2 percent of men.

Women's earnings as a percent of men's vary significantly by industry. In construction, where the gap is the smallest, women's earnings are 96.5 percent of men's. Women earn 86.4 percent of what men do in leisure and hospitality, and 83.2 percent of men's earnings in transportation and utilities. The earnings gap is largest in agriculture and related industries, where women's median weekly earnings are 47.3 percent of men's. Financial activities also has a large pay gap between genders, with women earning 69.2 percent of what men do.

Origin of the Wage Gap

Is this persistent wage gap an example of gender bias? A remnant of the good old boys club? Or is it a matter of economics and personal choice? It is probably a combination of discrimination and personal choice that perpetuates the wage gap. One argument, articulated by Hunter College psychology and linguistics professor Virginia Valian, says that the wage gap is a result of "gender schemas" in the workforce, implicit assumptions about gender differences—held by everyone— that create small differences in characteristics, behaviors, perceptions and evaluations of men and women, causing men to be constantly overrated in their professional lives, and women to be underrated.

Another argument is the glass ceiling; women seem to have more difficulty reaching the top ranks of any industry than do men, evidenced by the still-small ranks of female CEOs at major companies. In 2006, only 10 Fortune 500 companies had female CEOs, and only 20 Fortune 1000 CEOs were women.

Women are more heavily represented in office and administrative support occupations (24.9% of women and 6.8% of men), which tend to have lower wages.

Then there is the argument of choice. Women work part-time more often than men (25.2% and 10.7%, respectively). While this doesn't affect median weekly earnings, which accounted for only full-time year-round workers, it could affect the likelihood of promotions and the perceptions of future employers, thus affecting the wages of women who return to work full-time. Women also tend to take more breaks from employment during their careers, more frequently leaving the labor force to care for children and family responsibilities.

The argument has also been made that women are not drawn to the type of work that can come with high-risk premiums, including certain types of construction and protective service occupations. Less than 1 percent of women are in construction occupations and 11 percent of men are in construction, and just 1 percent of women are in protective service, while 3 percent of men are. Women are more heavily represented in office and administrative support occupations (24.9% of women and 6.8% of men), which tend to have lower wages.

Women's participation in the labor force stabilized in the first part of this decade [2000–2009]. Their labor force participation rate rose from 43.3 percent in 1970 to 59.3 percent in 2005, converging with men's participation rate, which dropped from 79.7 percent to 73.3 percent. Women have seen larger gains in their median weekly earnings over time, with women's earnings increasing 221 percent between 1970 and 2005 and men's increasing 147 percent. However, even with improvement over time, and regardless of the causes of the earnings gap, such a gap persists today.

The Wage Gap Between Men and Women Persists

Kristin Rowe-Finkbeiner

Kristin Rowe-Finkbeiner is the author of The F-Word: Feminism in Jeopardy—Women, Politics, and the Future, *and writes frequently about public policy and women's issues.*

The truth is American women are losing economic ground. The U.S. Census Bureau reported in August 2004 that the wage gap between men and women is increasing. In 2002, American women made 76.6 cents for every dollar made by men, and in 2003 that number dropped another penny. . . .

Is the wage gap really that significant? Do men really *need* to make more as "bread winners," as many assume?. . .

It's quite often assumed that if the woman works at all, her income isn't primary, or sorely needed by the family unit.

But this assumption simply doesn't play out in *most* modern households. Contemporary facts paint a different picture and show changing family and household dynamics. In 2003, only 23 percent of all American households consisted of married couples living with their children. Another 9 percent of all households consisted of a single-parent family. This means that a full 77 percent of households aren't made up of married couples with children.

The *Leave It to Beaver* stereotype simply doesn't fit. Times have changed. In fact, there were more one-person households in 2003 than households of married couples with children. And of those one-person households, a whopping 58 percent were women. . . .

Even for women in modern married-couple family situations, the main "bread winner" argument doesn't always work. This is quite simply because most families need two parents in the labor force in order to stay economically viable.

One shouldn't forget that many families who choose to have a stay-at-home parent take big economic hits. Contrary to popular belief that all stay-at-home parents are wealthy, families with a stay-at-home parent are about seven times more likely to live in poverty than those with two full-time working parents, according to a U.S. Census study. . . .

In 2001, a full one-quarter of families with children under age six lived in poverty and earned less than $25,000 annually. At federal minimum wage, a two-parent family will earn only $21,424 a year with both parents working full-time—and this is in a country where childcare can cost anywhere from $4,000 to $10,000 a year per child. Don't even bring up health-care costs and coverage. When you do the math, it's easy to see why so many families live in poverty.

Not surprisingly, most mothers do work outside of the home. Between July 2001 and July 2002, almost three-quarters of mothers with children past one year of age were in the labor force, about the same number as women without children. . . .

Certainly not all families, or women, live in poverty. Some are doing quite well: 5.2 percent of all top earners at Fortune 500 companies are women. Success stories are out there, but 5 percent "does not, shall we say, represent" the full picture of women wage earners—particularly when compared to the fact that women now comprise 47 percent of the entire paid labor force.

Dollars and Sense

"My company compensates me less than half of what the man who had my job before me made. When I confronted my boss with the issue, he told me to take it or leave it. I've also noticed that when a man comes in to represent a territory for my company, they give all existing accounts to the man, but when a woman starts out in the territory, they do not give her the bigger existing accounts, and she is instructed to work to find new business," says Roxanne, 28, who also responded to the social-issues survey for *The F-Word*.

A General Accounting Office (GAO) report . . . demonstrated no improvement in the pay gap between men and women over the past two decades.

Does this woman sound like she's whining? Maybe it's her fault that she isn't making the same wages? Maybe she misunderstood the wages and structure of her job? Because gender inequality is often assumed to be an old issue long-solved, women are frequently portrayed as complaining, or even whining, when they note wage disparities.

Sad to say, gender inequality is far from a thing of the past. In November 2003, U.S. Representatives Carolyn Maloney (D-NY) and John Dingell (D-MI) released the results of *Women's Earnings*, a General Accounting Office (GAO) report that demonstrated no improvement in the pay gap between men and women over the past two decades, despite a feeling of "continued progress toward gender equality in the workplace." Feelings are great, but they don't put food on the table.

Some people allege that the wage gap is influenced by women working fewer hours or by other "self-inflicted" factors. The GAO study controlled for outside variables such as education and work experience that could skew wage-gap calculations and still found a very significant gender wage gap.

The GAO study, which included 18 years of data on over 9,300 Americans and accounted for factors such as occupation, industry, race, marital status and job tenure in calculating comparable wages, concluded that a significant pay gap exists today. And while it points to a slightly smaller wage gap than the U.S. Census calculation, the GAO study still found that women made only 79 cents for every dollar paid to men.

When the GAO study factored out variables that may affect earnings, it found that women on average earned about 44 percent less than men between 1983 and 2000. In other words, if we put aside differences that affect earnings, such as education and employment interruptions, women actually earn far less than the calculated 79 percent of men's wages.

The Invisible Inequality

It's often difficult for individuals to see gender-based wage inequality. Generally, people don't compare their paychecks at the water fountain, and questioning why one person makes more than another is far from common. In fact, Amy Caiazza, Ph.D., study director for the Institute for Women's Policy Research notes, "Right now, in many instances, you can be fired for disclosing your salary. That means most people don't know what their co-workers are making. It's generally very difficult to know whether you are being discriminated against."

Caiazza continues with a solution to the problem. "There is a bill on Capitol Hill that would protect people so they won't be fired for talking about how much money they make. The bill also requires companies to analyze their salaries and wages and to disclose that data so potential patterns of discrimination can be seen. This is a very simple thing to do."

Regardless of how the data is analyzed, it's clear that over the past several decades, progress toward female-male wage parity has been slow—and it's been slowest for women of color who face both gender- and race-based discrimination. According to *The American Woman: 2003–2004*, white women experienced a 32 percent increase in median annual earnings from 1975 to 2000, while African-American women gained only 22 percent and Hispanic women just 12 percent.

Societal Trends

Societal trends are easier to see when large numbers of workers' wages are considered at the same time. That's when patterns show through the individual paychecks. In 2001, six current and former female Wal-Mart employees filed a national sex-discrimination class-action lawsuit, alleging widespread gender bias against women with regard to pay, job assignments and promotions. This lawsuit (*Dukes v. Wal-Mart Stores, Inc.*) is ongoing and active. Wal-Mart, the nation's largest private employer, has more than 3,000 stores around the country, and as many as 1.6 million women have worked for Wal-Mart since 1998.

What we're seeing . . . is the result of thousands of independent and individual decisions, combining to reveal the sexism within our culture and corporate system.

According to a statistical report prepared by the plaintiffs' expert, Dr. Richard Drogin, "Women employees at Wal-Mart are concentrated in the lower paying jobs, are paid less than men in the same jobs and are less likely to advance to management positions than men. These gender patterns persist even though women have more seniority, have lower turnover rates, and have higher performance ratings in most jobs."

Even more startling data emerged in a September 2003 oral argument by the plaintiffs' attorney, Brad Seligman, when he sought to elevate the case to class-action status. The following is an excerpt:

> It's also undisputed on this record that female retail store employees, hourly and salaried, separate or together are paid less than men in every year since 1996—and in every region of Wal-Mart, and that female employees, on average, are paid less than male employees in virtually every major job position in the retail store.

Seligman, executive director of the Impact Fund and lead counsel against Wal-Mart, analyzes Wal-Mart's response to the allegations: "Wal-Mart's defense is really to argue that there are 3,600 separate Wal-Marts, and not one national corporation. Interestingly, they didn't refute most of the evidence we put in, including stereotyping and bias at the top levels or Wal-Mart's knowledge of the discriminatory impacts."

Wal-Mart certainly doesn't have a national policy directing employees to "promote only men and pay them better while you're at it." What we're seeing instead is the result of thousands of independent and individual decisions, combining to reveal the sexism within our culture and corporate system.

Some might be saying, "Maybe the men were promoted because they were better managers at Wal-Mart?" In this case, it's important to note that according to a meta-analysis study published in the American Psychological Association (APA) *Psychological Bulletin* in 2003, on average, women in management positions are somewhat better leaders than men in equivalent positions.

A close look at the numbers shows the reason the wage gap is so large for all women is because the vast majority of American women are mothers.

This study, together with the higher job-performance ratings for women at Wal-Mart, effectively negates the question of whether men—at 3,000 stores—were more heavily promoted because they all "just happened" to be better managers. . . .

The Big Step: Motherhood

Yet, it's with motherhood—a time when families need more economic support for basic needs, childcare and health care, not less support—that women take the biggest economic hit these days. Motherhood also offers some clues as to how the wage gap can be narrowed.

Hold on to your hats: The wage gap between mothers and nonmothers under age 35 is now greater than that between women and men, and it has actually widened since the 1980s.

Jane Waldfogel at Columbia University studied the issue and found that the pay gap between mothers and nonmothers expanded from 10 percent in 1980 to 17.5 percent in 1991. Waldfogel's research focused on men and women with an average age of 30. She found that in 1980, mothers earned 56 percent of men's salaries, while nonmothers earned 66 percent. But by 1991, nonmothers' earnings had rocketed to 90.1 percent, while mothers earned only 72.6 percent.

A close look at the numbers shows the reason the wage gap is so large for all women is because the vast majority of American women are mothers. (In the year 2000, 82 percent of women had children by the time they were forty-four.) In other words, the majority of American women, mothers, are making less than the current average of 75.5 cents to a man's dollar, and the wages of nonmothers are actually bringing up this overall average.

The data . . . shows that men don't take wage hits after having children.

Waldfogel notes that the issue is more urgent for single mothers. They face a wage gap that has actually worsened relative to men and other women over the past few decades. "Single mothers now earn only 56–66 percent of what men earn, substantially less than women who are married mothers or not mothers at all," according to Waldfogel.

Again, critics often allege that the women in these studies may have had less education or work experience, thus skewing the findings. However, the study filtered the data to account for education and work experience. The data further shows that men don't take wage hits after having children. Something is really going on here.

And that "something" has a tremendous impact on poverty rates for women and families. Caiazza, from the Institute for Women's Policy Research, notes, "We did a study that found [that] if there wasn't a wage gap, the poverty rates for single moms would be cut in half, and the poverty rates for dual-earner families would be cut by about 25 percent."

This brings us to the heart of the matter—and to some ideas for solutions. One reason for the widening American wage gap is that U.S. policy has "emphasized equal pay and equal opportunity policies, but not family policies such as maternity leave and childcare," writes Waldfogel in the *Journal of Economic Perspectives*. Family policies such as paid family leave, as well as subsidized child and health care, have been shown to help close the gap in other countries.

Mentoring Does Not Narrow the Wage Gap

Sandie Taylor

Sandie Taylor has a doctorate in psychology and is a senior lecturer at Bathspa University in the United Kingdom.

For many MBA students, success means a big salary and an upwardly mobile career. But many female MBAs continue to experience a disparity in compensation and career advancement.

Despite comprising 47 percent of the non-agriculture work force and boasting higher college graduation rates than men since 1982, women take home only 76 percent of what males earn. More striking, only 15 percent of women hold top positions as board members or CEOs [chief executive officers] at Fortune 500 companies—numbers that have scarcely changed in a decade.

Mentorship is often prescribed as a tool to close this gender gap. Mentors help protégés develop competencies, learn norms of corporate culture, introduce them to important individuals, and provide emotional support and encouragement. Historically, women haven't enjoyed access to mentors in the same way as men have. But as women entered the corporate work force in greater numbers over the last 15 years, both the media and corporate managers averred the connections and guidance a mentor provides would help women advance.

That prediction hasn't panned out. According to Paul V. Martorana, assistant professor of management at the Mc-Combs School of Business at the University of Texas at Austin; Jeanne M. Brett, professor of dispute resolution and organizations at the Kellogg School of Management at North-

Sandie Taylor, "Equal Opportunities?" *Exchange*, 2007, pp. 22–23. Reproduced by permission of McCombs School of Business at The University of Texas at Austin.

western University; and Catherine H. Tinsley, associate professor of management at the McDonough School of Business at Georgetown University, the mere presence of a career mentor does not consistently help women break through the glass ceiling when it comes to achieving pay equity and attaining executive roles.

In their study, "The Persistent Gender Gap Among Protégés," Martorana and his colleagues, Jeanne Brett of Northwestern University and Catherine Tinsley of Georgetown University, find the gap has generally stayed the same. And in some cases, despite the presence of mentors, the income disparity between men and women has increased.

Widening the Wage Gap

In a field study of 641 alumni from a Midwestern law school and business school, Martorana found that mentorship had an overall positive effect on the careers of both men and women. The researchers examined compensation (including salary and bonuses) of MBA graduates from their initial salaries after completing their MBAs to five years after graduation.

The results, which are described in the working paper, "Mentoring and the Gender Gap: Women's Satisfaction and Men's Career Advancement" showed that females without mentors reported an average compensation increase of $36,765, whereas females with mentors earned $65,742 more than they had five years prior. However, for men, those without mentors reported an average increase of $57,067, and those with mentors earned $79,336 more after five years. In addition, women with mentors did not even earn as much ($132,399) as men without mentors ($139,078).

As far as promotions go, both men and women with mentors gained more promotions than those who did not have mentors. But again, men with mentors received significantly more promotions than women with mentors did.

"There's a benefit to having a mentor," says Martorana, a member of the steering committee of The University of Texas at Austin's Center for Women and Gender Studies. Both genders gain more promotions and financial compensation when they have mentors, he says, but the rate of salary growth and promotions between men and women has not equalized. "Women feel like they are being brought into the fold, but it's not happening," he adds. "It's not even helping women gain equality."

These results reflect a national trend. Within the last 10 years, the pay gap has not improved for college-educated women—in fact, the difference in earning power is greater today than it was a decade ago. According to a recent study by the Labor Department's Economic Policy Institute, in 2005, college-educated women between 36 and 45 years old earned 74.7 cents in hourly pay for every dollar that men in the same group did. A decade earlier, women earned 75.7 cents to the dollar compared to men.

Past research on women's career choices find that stereotypes may explain this stagnation. A 1999 study published in the *Journal of Management Inquiry* reported that although women are perceived to be less interested in making risky career moves, female managers were, in fact, no less willing to relocate for work than male managers. Moreover, women did not turn down relocation offers more frequently than males— they were simply offered fewer relocation opportunities. In addition, the study showed that female managers were just as likely to seek employment outside of their firms as male managers. But women who were offered external positions were compensated with few benefits, whereas male managers benefited greatly, especially financially.

Even more discouraging is the fact that the United States seems to be lagging behind its international peers. Two years ago [in 2006], the World Economic Forum released the *Global*

Gender Gap Report 2006 with a list of the top 10 countries that are closest to achieving gender equality. The U.S. is conspicuously absent.

A Good Mentor Is Hard to Find

As other countries get closer to achieving equality, it's hard to say exactly why the U.S. gap has widened slightly in recent years. Research shows that even though more women are working in corporate America, it's still difficult for women to find mentors.

"There may be the unfair perception that women will not become stars, and so others may not want to mentor them." Martorana says.

In some organizations, the only employees chosen for mentorship experiences are "fast-track" individuals, and women are less likely to be considered part of that group. There's also the obvious problem of having fewer women at the top available to mentor other females (although Martorana's study examined women who had both male and female mentors). Women's relatively sparse professional networks tend to limit the opportunity for referrals.

Having a mentor can bring many rewards—but much work remains before the glass ceiling becomes a thing of the past.

Women in senior management positions have the most trouble. "They're always providing support but often don't have other women above to mentor them," Martorana suggests. In addition, women in upper management benefit from mentorship with salary growth but do not receive nearly as many promotions as mentored men or even mentored females in lower management.

Martorana says this appears to be due to a glass ceiling effect. "The top managers probably have a difficult time finding someone [male or female] to tell them what is needed to get promotions," he says. "Or it could have something to do with when the [manager] got the job and how long she had been in upper management." A woman hired into a high-level position may receive raises but not the highest level promotions, he adds.

Studies have also shown that men avoid mentoring females for a variety of reasons, including concerns about the perception of sexual innuendo and limited understanding of women's challenges.

"Sexual innuendo is a big one," Martorana explains. "Men may not feel comfortable closing the door [for private conversations with women], and they can't chat with them in the locker room or men's room either."

Solutions for Success

So why are the results of mentorship so different for women and men? Martorana suggests men and women may have different relationships with a mentor. Whereas men may discuss career advancement-related issues and actually talk about real salary numbers, women may spend more time discussing social issues, such as work-life balance or relationships with a boss or co-worker.

The silver lining to the gender gap cloud may be the psychosocial support women get from mentors, which may have resulted in their increased job satisfaction. Women reported being slightly more satisfied with their mentorship experiences than men were despite the findings that mentored women may not receive the same quality of relationship as their male peers.

As women continue to seek mentors, it seems other solutions are still needed if women are to reach equal ground with men.

"Reducing the pay gap between men and women is a difficult project that requires constant vigilance," Martorana says.

He says one approach to closing the gap might be for organizations to focus on de-institutionalizing the barriers that women face with a "gendered" work environment. For example, companies could use training programs to educate employees about research that disproves gender stereotypes, such as perceived differences between women's and men's rationality and emotional stability.

"Another organization consideration is to discontinue the common practice of increasing compensation as a percent of an employee's initial or existing compensation," he says. "Giving raises or bonuses that are a percent of existing compensation—rather than a lump sum amount—simply perpetuates the gender differences that persist from when one enters the organization."

And instead of scrapping mentorship programs altogether, Martorana says companies might examine their goals for such programs. If the company is hoping to help women succeed, it could make its goals of the mentoring program explicit. That is, companies should not assume that mentors and protégés will always seek or provide the kind of help that results in career advancement or gender equality.

"If they want to improve protégés' chances for promotions or if they want to reduce the gender wage gap for women protégés, then they should explicitly let mentors and protégés know that they should work towards those goals," he says. "If they want to improve protégés' job satisfaction and feelings of belonging then they should make that goal explicit."

Though men continue to earn significantly more than women and hold more of the top corporate positions, the women in this sample do appear to be more satisfied with their jobs. While the gender gap persists, increased job satisfaction is not an insignificant achievement.

Martorana's research makes clear that mentorship has not yet succeeded in bridging the gender gap. Having a mentor can bring many rewards—but much work remains before the glass ceiling becomes a thing of the past.

College-Educated Women Struggle to Even the Wage Gap

Judy Goldberg Dey and Catherine Hill

Judy Goldberg Dey is an independent researcher with the American Association of University Women (AAUW) Educational Foundation. Catherine Hill is the AAUW Educational Foundation director of research.

Women have made remarkable gains in education during the past three decades, yet these achievements have resulted in only modest improvements in pay equity. The gender pay gap has become a fixture of the U.S. workplace and is so ubiquitous that many simply view it as normal. . . .

One year out of college, women working full time earn only 80 percent as much as their male colleagues earn. Ten years after graduation, women fall farther behind, earning only 69 percent as much as men earn. Controlling for hours, occupation, parenthood, and other factors normally associated with pay, college-educated women still earn less than their male peers earn.

Choices and Earning Potential

Individuals can, however, make choices that can greatly enhance their earnings potential. Choosing to attend college and completing a college degree have strong positive effects on earnings, although all college degrees do not have the same effect. The selectivity of the college attended and the choice of a major also affect later earnings. Many majors remain strongly dominated by one gender. Female students are concentrated in fields associated with lower earnings, such as education, health, and psychology. Male students dominate the higher-paying fields: engineering, mathematics, and physical sciences. Women and men who majored in "male-dominated" subjects earn more than do those who majored in "female-dominated" or "mixed-gender" fields. For example, one year after graduation, the average female education major working full time earns only 60 percent as much as the average female engineering major working full time earns.

The choice of major is not the full story, however. As early as one year after graduation, a pay gap is found between women and men who had the same college major. In education, a female-dominated major, women earn 95 percent as much as their male colleagues earn. In biological sciences, a mixed-gender major, women earn only 75 percent as much as men earn. Likewise in mathematics—a male-dominated major—women earn only 76 percent as much as men earn. Female students cannot simply choose a major that will allow them to avoid the pay gap.

Early career choices, most prominently occupational choices, also play a role in the gender pay gap. While the choice of major is related to occupation, the relationship is not strict. For example, some mathematics majors choose to teach, while others work in business or computer science. One year after graduation, women who work in computer science, for instance, earn over 37 percent more than do women who are employed in education or administrative, clerical, or legal support occupations. Job sector also affects earnings. Women are more likely than men to work in the nonprofit and local government sectors, where wages are typically lower than those in the for-profit and federal government sectors.

Parenthood and the Wage Gap

The division of labor between parents appears to be similar to that of previous generations. Motherhood and fatherhood affect careers differently. Mothers are more likely than fathers (or other women) to work part time, take leave, or take a break from the work force—factors that negatively affect wages. Among women who graduated from college in 1992–93, more than one-fifth (23 percent) of mothers were out of the work force in 2003, and another 17 percent were working part time. Less than 2 percent of fathers were out of the work force in 2003, and less than 2 percent were working part time. On average, mothers earn less than women without children earn and both groups earn less than men earn.

Motherhood in our society entails substantial economic and personal sacrifices. Fatherhood, on the other hand, appears to engender a "wage premium."

The gender pay gap among full-time workers understates the real difference between women's and men's earnings because it excludes women who are not in the labor force or who are working part time. Most college-educated women who are not working full time will eventually return to the full-time labor market. On average, these women will then have lower wages than will their continuously employed counterparts, further widening the pay gap.

What can be done about the gender pay gap? To begin with, it must be publicly recognized as a problem. Too often, both women and men dismiss the pay gap as simply a matter of different choices, but even women who make the same occupational choices that men make will not typically end up with the same earnings. Moreover, if "too many" women make the same choice, earnings in that occupation can be expected to decline overall.

Women's personal choices are similarly fraught with inequities. The difference between motherhood and fatherhood is particularly stark. Motherhood in our society entails substantial economic and personal sacrifices. Fatherhood, on the other hand, appears to engender a "wage premium." Indeed, men appear to spend more time at the office after becoming a father, whereas women spend considerably less time at work after becoming a mother. Women who do not have children may still be viewed as "potential mothers" by employers, who may, as a result, give women fewer professional opportunities.

Ideally, women and men should have similar economic opportunities and equal opportunities to enjoy meaningful unpaid work, such as parenting. Improving women's earnings could have positive consequences for men who would like to spend more time with their children but who can't afford to reduce their work hours. Likewise, workplace accommodations for parenting could be valuable for fathers as well as mothers. Other groups may also benefit from greater flexibility in the workplace, including older workers seeking "partial retirement," students hoping to combine work with study, and workers with other kinds of caregiving responsibilities.

Discrimination and the Wage Gap

The pay gap between female and male college graduates cannot be fully accounted for by factors known to affect wages, such as experience (including work hours), training, education, and personal characteristics. Gender pay discrimination can be overt or it can be subtle. It is difficult to document because someone's gender is usually easily identified by name, voice, or appearance. The only way to discover discrimination is to eliminate the other possible explanations. . . .

Women's progress throughout the past 30 years attests to the possibility of change. Before Title VII of the Civil Rights Act of 1964 and Title IX of the Education Amendments of 1972, employers could—and did—refuse to hire women for occupations deemed "unsuitable," fire women when they became pregnant, or limit women's work schedules on the basis of gender. Schools could—and did—set quotas for the number of women admitted or refuse women admission altogether. In the decades since these civil rights laws were enacted, women have made remarkable progress in fields such as law, medicine, and business as well as some progress in nontraditional "blue-collar" jobs such as aviation and firefighting.

Despite the progress women have made, gender pay equity in the workplace remains an issue. Improvements to federal equal pay laws are needed to ensure that women and men are compensated fairly when they perform the same or comparable work. Flexibility, meaningful part-time work opportunities, and expanded provisions for medical and family leave are important to help women and men better balance work and family responsibilities. Making gender pay equity a reality will require action by individuals, employers, and federal and state governments.

CHAPTER 2

What Is Causing the Wage Gap Between the Rich and the Poor?

Chapter Preface

Wal-Mart is the world's largest public corporation by revenue, the world's largest private employer, and the largest grocery retailer in the United States. The success of Wal-Mart is astounding. However, the retailer's success is often overshadowed with criticism for paying employees low wages and inadequate benefits. Supporters of Wal-Mart argue that the company is a free-market success story that has offered jobs and opportunities to thousands. The impact that the successful retailer has on the rich-poor wage gap is debatable.

Critics of Wal-Mart argue that the retailer does not pay its employees a living wage. A living wage is the minimum hourly wage necessary for a person to afford housing, food, utilities, transportation, health care, and recreation. According to the Ithaca Wal-Mart Living Wage Campaign, since Wal-Mart's entry into the grocery business, wages and benefits of those working in supermarkets have declined by 14 percent, averaging out to those employees earning a dollar less each hour. Critics of Wal-Mart accuse the retailer of predator pricing, which is when a firm sells a product at a very low price, often below cost, with the intent of driving competitors out of the market. Once the competition is driven out of the market, the predator can then raise its prices above market value. Predatory pricing leads to fewer benefits and lower wages paid to employees of not only the retailer but also employees of its suppliers and competition.

The health plan offered by Wal-Mart is inadequate and impacts taxpayers, according to the United Food and Commercial Workers Union. In January 2006, Wal-Mart reported that its health insurance only covered 43 percent of its 1.39 million U.S. employees. Many Wal-Mart employees are not eligible for company benefits because they work part-time. The remaining Wal-Mart employees who are eligible for medical benefits do not accept the company's benefit plans because they find the premiums and medical deductibles too expensive. As a result, taxpayers pay the cost indirectly. Ithaca Wal-Mart Living Wage Campaign estimates the total cost to taxpayers nationally for public assistance to Wal-Mart employees and their families could be as much as $2 billion a year.

Many argue that Wal-Mart should not be faulted for paying low wages. Low wages earned by retail employees is nothing new. "Front-line service-sector employees have never made livable wages," says Jim Hoopes, professor of business ethics at Babson College in Wellesley, MA, "or at least they have always been among the most poorly paid." Others argue that Wal-Marts are located in just about every community in the United States, creating jobs and opportunities for those who would otherwise be unemployed. Thousands of small towns across America have seen boosts to their local economy after the opening of a Wal-Mart.

Supporters of Wal-Mart also label the retailer as a free-market success story, striving to improve customers' living standards through low prices. An independent study by Global Insight, a privately held economic analysis company, found that Wal-Mart saved each American household, on average, $2,329 in 2004. Many say the success of Wal-Mart is due to Wal-Mart founder Sam Walton's business strategy. Walton realized that by offering customers discount prices he could make more profits based on increased volume. In the past, small-town retailers faced competition from the development of the railroad, the Sears catalog, and shopping malls. Retailers that have survived in the past were able to adapt to the changing retail market. Supporters of Wal-Mart say that retailers that find themselves in competition with Wal-Mart today have the same opportunity to adapt and even thrive once a Wal-Mart opens in their community.

According to Floyd J. McKay of the *Seattle Times*, "We live in a nation in which the real-dollar income of an average family has declined for years, while corporate profits and executive pay have skyrocketed." McKay believes Wal-Mart contributes to the rich-poor wage gap by exploiting the poor. Others oppose McKay's view, noting the positive impacts Wal-Mart has made toward the rich-poor wage gap. An October 2003 *Business Week* article noted that Wal-Mart's cost efficiency has contributed to economy-wide productivity gains and reduced the annual rate of inflation by about one percentage point. On the other hand, Wal-Mart has been blamed for the loss of U.S. manufacturing jobs and the closure of small-town local shops. The presence of the rich-poor wage gap is apparent; however, its causes are debatable. The following articles further explore possible factors that contribute to the rich-poor wage gap.

Income Inequality Has Widened the Wage Gap Between Rich and Poor

John Edward

John Edward is an adjunct professor of economics at Bentley College in Massachusetts.

LeBron James, the basketball star, is having a 35,000-square-foot mansion built for himself in suburban Ohio. It includes a barbershop. One out of every five people in the city of Lowell [Massachusetts] live in poverty. Some do without a haircut because they cannot afford one. Presidential candidate John Edwards observes these two Americas, so it is ironic when he pays $400 for a haircut for himself.

Inequality in America

Inequality has always existed, and always will. However, the gap between the rich and the poor is growing to alarming levels. While a select few are accumulating unimaginable wealth, many working families cannot imagine how they will pay their bills.

The trend is obvious from looking at United States Census data. After a long period of decreasing inequality, the United States has experienced a steady increase in inequality over the past 30 years.

In the mid 1970s, high-income families earned seven times as much as low-income families. Now they earn 12 times as much. Back then, the top 1 percent of earners made 9 percent of total income. Now they make 19 percent.

An extensive study of federal tax returns confirms this dramatic trend. In 1980, the top one-hundredth of one per-

John Edward, "Income Inequality Continues to Grow," *The Lowell* (MA) *Sun*, September 9, 2007, p. 1. Reproduced by permission.

cent of income earners received 1 percent of all income. By 2005, the same group was making 5 percent of all income. The "poorest" of these families made $9.5 million in 2005.

This is not the first time the United States has experienced a huge income gap. We had inequality like this a little over a century ago during the Gilded Age. The robber barons of the time built luxurious mansions and estates (some with private barbershops perhaps). The same tax return study shows a spike in inequality similar to the one we have now. It was in the 1920s—just before the Great Depression.

The aptly titled *Fortune* magazine looked at the 100 highest paid chief executive officers. In 1970, their average pay was $1.3 million per year, or about 40 times that of the average worker. By 2000, the top 100 were making $37.5 million per year, or 1000 times what a typical worker made.

Few would begrudge rewarding someone for running a successful company. However, pay-for-performance is a myth. Warren Buffet devoted an entire section of his 2006 shareholder letter to executive pay. He described the compensation paid to "mediocre-or-worse CEOs" as "ridiculously out of line."

While some thrive, Community Teamwork Inc. [CTI] assists people in Greater Lowell who think in terms of survival. CTI offers a variety of services designed to help people become self-sufficient. However, many area residents are working hard and losing ground. Some do not earn enough to make ends meet. Some work multiple jobs.

Directors at CTI report an increase in the number of people seeking shelter. They described the situation to me as aspiring first to make people feel safe, and then stable, and maybe someday, to thrive.

Causes of Inequality

The problem is that trickle down economics is not working. The Congressional Budget Office reports that in the 25-year period ending in 2004, incomes for the top 1 percent increased by 157 percent (adjusted for inflation). High-income earners did quite well with a 63 percent gain. Middle-income households did less well—a 15 percent increase. Low-income households increased by only 2 percent. For the top 1 percent, income gains could be in millions of dollars, while for low-income households we are talking about hundreds of dollars.

The trend is even more dramatic in our neighborhood [New England]. A recent University of New Hampshire study looked at increasing income inequality by region. New England is showing the largest increase in the gap between rich and poor.

In Massachusetts, wages for low-income families have actually gone down. Our "Commonwealth" is now one of the most unequal states according to MassINC, a nonpartisan research organization.

Studies by the Federal Reserve Bank of Boston and the Bureau of Labor Statistics show that income mobility is decreasing in the United States.

The increasing inequality trend is evident in Lowell. Data from the 2000 census shows that the median income in Belvidere was around $60,000. In one section of the Acre, the median income was less than $10,000. One study identified Lowell as the urban area in the United States with the largest increase in income inequality in the 1980s. As with the rest of the nation, the gap has continued to grow.

Another trend is compounding the problem. Studies by the Federal Reserve Bank of Boston and the Bureau of Labor Statistics show that income mobility is decreasing in the United States. Low-income earners are more likely to stay that way.

The trend of increasing inequality is obvious when you look at the numbers. However, the reasons for this trend are not so clear. There is a big income gap based on education and training. Technology has made this gap even larger. Globalization has resulted in many low-paying jobs moving overseas. The jobs that stay pay less. Unions have diminished in membership and influence. The minimum wage has fallen significantly when adjusted for inflation. Tax cuts during the past 30 years have greatly favored the wealthy.

In Massachusetts, our tax structure promotes inequality. The poor pay a much higher tax rate than the wealthy when you factor in all state and local taxes. We are transferring money from the poor to the rich in a reverse Robin Hood paradox.

The Economy and Inequality

There is no consensus as to what we should do about inequality, if anything. Some see inequality as a natural result of our market-based economy that has been growing at a strong pace. Yet, the economy grew faster back in the 1950s and '60s when incomes were much less unequal.

Lack of money often leads to inequities in education, health, and the legal system.

Some are very concerned that a rising tide is not lifting all boats, just the yachts. Is the American dream out of reach for many?

What is clear is that inequality is increasing and has increased to levels not seen in a long time. This should be a genuine cause for dismay for low-income families, or those concerned with fairness. Lack of money often leads to inequities in education, health, and the legal system.

There is another reason why we should all be worried about increasing inequality. If inequality gets any worse, it may slow down economic growth; it could be doing so already.

Further discussion on that will have to wait for another day.

Executives Earn Their High Salaries

Ira T. Kay

Ira T. Kay is global practice director for executive compensation at Watson Wyatt Worldwide and coauthor along with Steven Van Putten of the book Myths and Realities of Executive Pay.

For years, headlines have seized on dramatic accounts of outrageous amounts earned by executives—often of failing companies—and the financial tragedy that can befall both shareholders and employees when CEOs [chief executive officers] line their own pockets at the organization's expense. Images of lavish executive lifestyles are now engraved in the popular consciousness. The result: public support for political responses that include new regulatory measures and a long list of demands for greater shareholder or government control over executive compensation.

These images now overshadow the reality of thousands of successful companies with appropriately paid executives and conscientious boards. Instead, fresh accusations of CEOs collecting huge amounts of undeserved pay appear daily, fueling a full-blown mythology of a corporate America ruled by executive greed, fraud, and corruption.

This mythology consists of two related components: the myth of the failed pay-for-performance model and the myth of managerial power. The first myth hinges on the idea that the link between executive pay and corporate performance—if it ever existed—is irretrievably broken. The second myth accepts the idea of a failed pay-for-performance model and puts in its service the image of unchecked CEOs dominating subservient boards as the explanation for decisions resulting in

Ira T. Kay, "Don't Mess with CEO Pay," *Across the Board*, vol. 43, January/February 2006, pp. 23–28. Reproduced by permission.

excessive executive pay. The powerful combination of these two myths has captured newspaper headlines and shareholder agendas, regulatory attention and the public imagination. . . .

Fueling the Fiction

In recent years, dozens of reporters from business magazines and the major newspapers have called me and specifically asked for examples of companies in which CEOs received exorbitant compensation, approved by the board, while the company performed poorly. Not once have I been asked to comment on the vast majority of companies—those in which executives are appropriately rewarded for performance or in which boards have reduced compensation or even fired the CEO for poor performance.

Using CEOs as scapegoats distracts from the real causes of and possible solutions for inequality.

I have spent hundreds of hours answering reporters' questions, providing extensive data and explaining the pay-for-performance model of executive compensation, but my efforts have had little impact: The resulting stories feature the same anecdotal reporting on those corporations for which the process has gone awry. The press accounts ignore solid research that shows that annual pay for most executives moves up and down significantly with the company's performance, both financial and stock-related. Corporate wrongdoings and outlandish executive pay packages make for lively headlines, but the reliance on purely anecdotal reporting and the highly prejudicial language adopted are a huge disservice to the companies, their executives and employees, investors, and the public. The likelihood of real economic damage to the U.S. economy grows daily. . . .

The Return of Investment of the CEO

As with all modern myths, there's a grain of truth in all the assumptions and newspaper stories. The myths of managerial power and of the failed pay-for-performance model find touchstones in real examples of companies where CEOs have collected huge sums in cash compensation and stock options while shareholder returns declined. (You know the names—there's no need to mention them again here.) Cases of overstated profits or even outright fraud have fueled the idea that executives regularly manipulate the measures of performance to justify higher pay while boards default on their oversight responsibilities. The ability of executives to time the exercise of their stock options and collect additional pay through covert means has worsened perceptions of the situation both within and outside of the world of business.

These exceptions in executive pay practices, however, are now commonly mistaken for the rule. . . . Highly paid CEOs have become the new whipping boys for social critics concerned about the general rise in income inequality and other broad socioeconomic problems. Never mind that these same CEOs stand at the center of a corporate model that has generated millions of jobs and trillions of dollars in shareholder earnings. Worse, using CEOs as scapegoats distracts from the real causes of and possible solutions for inequality.

The primary determinant of CEO pay is the same force that sets pay for all Americans: relatively free—if somewhat imperfect—labor markets, in which companies offer the levels of compensation necessary to attract and retain the employees who generate value for shareholders. Part of that pay for most executives consists of stock-based incentives. A 2003 study by Brian J. Hall and Kevin J. Murphy shows that the ratio of total CEO compensation to production workers' average earnings closely follows the Dow Jones Industrial Average. When the Dow soars, the gap between executive and non-executive compensation widens. The problem, it seems, is not that CEOs receive too much performance-driven, stock-based compensation, but that non-executives receive too little.

I have never witnessed board members straining to find a way to pay an executive more than he is worth.

The key question is not the actual dollar amount paid to a CEO in total compensation or whether that amount represents a high multiple of pay of the average worker's salary but, rather, whether that CEO creates an adequate return on the company's investment in executive compensation. In virtually every area of business, directors routinely evaluate and adjust the amounts that companies invest in all inputs, and shareholders directly or indirectly endorse or challenge those decisions. Executive pay is no different.

Hard Realities

The corporate scandals of recent years laid bare the finer workings of a handful of public companies where, inarguably, the process for setting executive pay violated not only the principle of pay-for-performance but the extensive set of laws and regulations governing executive pay practices and the role of the board. But while I condemn illegal actions and criticize boards that reward executives who fail to produce positive financial results, I know that the vast majority of U.S. corporations do much better by their shareholders and the public. I have worked directly with more than a thousand publicly traded companies in the United States and attended thousands of compensation-committee meetings, and I have never witnessed board members straining to find a way to pay an executive more than he is worth.

In addition, at Watson Wyatt I work with a team of experts that has conducted extensive research at fifteen hundred of America's largest corporations and tracked the relationship between these pay practices and corporate performance over almost twenty years. In evaluating thousands of companies annually, yielding nearly twenty thousand "company years" of data, and pooling cross-sectional company data over multiple years, we have discovered that for both most companies and the "typical" company, there is substantial pay-for-performance sensitivity. That is, high performance generates high pay for executives and low performance generates low pay. Numerous empirical academic studies support our conclusions.

Our empirical evidence and evidence from other studies have produced the following key findings:

1. Executive pay is unquestionably high relative to low-level corporate positions, and it has risen dramatically over the past ten to fifteen years, faster than inflation and faster than average employee pay. But executive compensation generally tracks total returns to share-holders—even including the recent rise in pay.

2. Executive stock ownership has risen dramatically over the past ten to fifteen years. High levels of CEO stock ownership are correlated with and most likely the cause of companies' high financial and stock-market perfor-mance.

3. Executives are paid commensurate with the skills and talents that they bring to the organization. Underper-forming executives routinely receive pay reductions or are terminated—far more often than press accounts im-ply.

4. CEOs who are recruited from outside a company and have little influence over its board receive compensation that is competitive with and often higher than the pay levels of CEOs who are promoted from within the com-pany.

5. At the vast majority of companies, even extraordinarily high levels of CEO compensation represent a tiny frac-tion of the total value created by the corporation under

that CEO's leadership. (Watson Wyatt has found that U.S. executives receive approximately 1 percent of the net income generated by the corporations they manage.) Well-run companies, it bears pointing out, produce significant shareholder returns and job security for millions of workers.

Extensive research demonstrates a high and positive correlation between executive pay and corporate performance. For example, high levels of executive stock ownership in 2000, created primarily through stock-option awards, correlated with higher stock-market valuation and long-term earnings per share over the subsequent five-year period. In general, high-performing companies are led by highly paid executives—with pay-for-performance in full effect. Executives at low-performing companies receive lower amounts of pay. Reams of data from other studies confirm these correlations. . . .

Why CEOs Are Worth the Money

CEOs have significant, legitimate, market-driven bargaining power, and in pay negotiations, they use that power to obtain pay commensurate with their skills. Boards, as they should, use their own bargaining power to retain talent and maximize returns to company shareholders.

Many economists argue [that] the U.S. model of executive compensation is a significant source of competitive advantage for the nation's economy, driving higher productivity, profits, and stock prices.

Boards understand the imperative of finding an excellent CEO and are willing to risk millions of dollars to secure the right talent. Their behavior is not only understandable but necessary to secure the company's future success. Any influence that CEOs might have over their directors is modest in comparison to the financial risk that CEOs assume when they leave other prospects and take on the extraordinarily difficult task of managing a major corporation, with a substantial portion of their short- and long-term compensation contingent on the organization's financial success. . . .

Properly designed pay opportunities drive superior corporate performance and secure it for the future. And most importantly, many economists argue, the U.S. model of executive compensation is a significant source of competitive advantage for the nation's economy, driving higher productivity, profits, and stock prices.

Resetting the Debate

Companies design executive pay programs to accomplish the classic goals of any human-capital program. First, they must attract, retain, and motivate their human capital to perform at the highest levels. The motivational factor is the most important, because it addresses the question of how a company achieves the greatest return on its human-capital investment and rewards executives for making the right decisions to drive shareholder value. Incentive-pay and pay-at-risk programs are particularly effective, especially at the top of the house, in achieving this motivation goal.

Clearly, there are exceptions to the motivational element—base salaries, pensions, and other benefits, for example—that are more closely tied to retention goals and are an essential part of creating a balanced portfolio for the employee. The portfolio as a whole must address the need for income and security and the opportunity for creating significant asset appreciation.

In some ways, the decidedly negative attention focused on executive pay has increased the pressure that executives, board members, HR [human resources] staffs, and compensation consultants all feel when they enter into discussions about the most effective methods for tying pay to performance and ensuring the company's success. The managerial-power argument has contributed to meaningful discussions about corporate governance and raised the level of dialogue in boardrooms. These are positive developments.

When the argument is blown into mythological proportions, however, it skews thinking about the realities of corporate behavior and leads to fundamental misunderstandings about executives, their pay levels, and their role in building successful companies and a flourishing economy. Consequently, the mythology now surrounding executive compensation leads many to reject a pay model that works well and is critical to ongoing growth at both the corporate and the national economic level. We need to address excesses in executive pay without abandoning the core model, and to return the debate to a rational, informed discussion.

Foreign Competition and Technology Contribute to the Rich-Poor Wage Gap

David Wessel

David Wessel, the deputy chief of the Washington bureau of the Wall Street Journal, *writes a weekly column called "Capital."*

Much of the American anxiety about outsourcing to India and China can be boiled down to this simple question: Will there be good jobs left for our kids?

It's easy to see why there is so much concern. Tens of millions of increasingly skilled Chinese and Indian workers are joining the global economy at a moment when technology can dispatch white-collar work overseas almost instantly—from call centers to sophisticated design projects, the very jobs that discouraged U.S. factory workers hoped their children would get.

The good news: The U.S. almost certainly isn't going to run out of jobs, even though history shows that it's impossible to predict what new jobs will replace those that are destroyed. The bad news: Outsourcing overseas and technology could widen the gap between the wages of well-paying brainpower jobs and poorly paid hands-on jobs.

Jobs that can be reduced to a series of rules are likely to go—either to workers abroad or to computers. The jobs that stay in the U.S. or that are newly created in the decade ahead are likely to demand the more complex skill of recognizing patterns or require human contact.

The 25%-plus unemployment rates of the Great Depression are extremely unlikely to return as long as the U.S. has a capable Federal Reserve that can move interest rates, a president and Congress that will cut taxes and increase spending when the economy slides and a widely used currency that falls when necessary to make exports more attractive. After all, the "jobless recovery" of the early 1990s was followed by a stretch of the lowest unemployment in a generation.

Each generation considers its own time to be unique. Today's popular demon is foreign competition. Forty years ago, it was automation. In March 1964, three dozen liberal luminaries wrote Lyndon Johnson that "the combination of the computer and the automated self-regulating machine" was creating "almost unlimited productivity capacity which requires progressively less human labor." Without massive government spending, they warned, the U.S. would suffer mass joblessness and poverty.

Jobs will proliferate at both ends of the barbell—and fewer in the middle. The result would be an ever-wider gap between well-paying jobs and poorly paid jobs.

Since then, the U.S. economy has added 72 million jobs, an increase of 125%. Compared to a counterpart of the same age and schooling, the typical full-time male worker's wages have risen by 18% after adjusting for inflation; for women, wages are up 37%. Today's unemployment rate is almost exactly where it was in 1964. Computers in the factory and in the office have replaced humans. But jobs lost were replaced by jobs unimagined in 1964.

More jobs are bound to disappear. "If you can describe a job precisely, or write rules for doing it, it's unlikely to survive. Either we'll program a computer to do it, or we'll teach a foreigner to do it," says Frank Levy, a Massachusetts Institute of Technology economist. If a worker can respond to a baffled U.S. computer user by reading a script from a computer screen, that job will go to India. If voice-recognition software can field a magazine-subscription request, that job will go to a computer.

"Outsourcing accelerates what technology was already doing," Mr. Levy adds. "Take call centers. Eight, 10 years down the line, we could do a lot more with voice-recognition software. But with outsourcing you can do away with those jobs now."

New jobs surely will emerge to replace those lost. That's happened with every past breakthrough in technology and trade. "In 1940," observes chief White House economist Greg Mankiw, "no one could have predicted that some grandchildren of farmers would become Web-site designers and CAT-scan operators. But they did, and at much higher wages and incomes."

This time, two different kinds of jobs are likely to flourish amid outsourcing and computerization.

One sort requires physical contact—nursing-home aides, janitors, gardeners, dentists. Foreign-born workers may do them, but they'll have to move to the U.S. A 2000 survey found that the average starting salary of graduates of community-college dental-hygiene programs was $41,900.

A hot program at many community colleges these days is massage therapy. Springfield Technical Community College in western Massachusetts gets nearly 50 applications each year for the 20 slots in its six-year-old program, nearly all of them from women. Graduates earn an associate's degree and haven't had any trouble finding work, says Bernadette Bitta Nicholson, who runs the program. About a third go to work for local spas, which give therapists half of the $80 an hour charge for a massage. Another third find work at local health-care facilities and the remainder go into business for themselves.

The other sort of jobs destined to remain here are high-end jobs. Some require exchanging information in ways that e-mail and teleconferencing don't handle well. Think about teaching first grade or selling a mansion to a multimillionaire or conceiving new forms of software. Others demand such intimate knowledge of the U.S. that it's hard to see foreigners doing them from afar. Think about marketing to American teenagers or lobbying Congress.

Precisely identifying jobs that will replace those now disappearing is impossible. The Bureau of Labor Statistics [BLS], as good as anyone at this exercise, shows just how difficult it is.

In 1988, the agency predicted that the number of gas-station attendants would rise from 308,000 to 331,000 in 2000. When 2000 arrived, there were only 140,000. "Most gas stations are now self-service only," BLS economists Andrew Alpert and Jill Auyer explained in a candid retrospective the agency published. The BLS didn't see that coming.

In 1988, the BLS also projected travel agents would be among the 20 fastest-growing occupations, their ranks growing by 54% by 2000. Wrong again. The number of travel agents fell by 6.2%. Government prognosticators foresaw an increase in travel—but not the explosion of online booking.

Of 20 occupations that the BLS predicted in 1988 would suffer the greatest losses between 1988 and 2000, half actually grew. The agency predicted that the number of assemblers in electrical and electronic factories would drop by 173,000, a 44% decrease. Twelve years later, there were 45,000 more, an 11% increase. Neither outsourcing nor robots made as much of a dent as the BLS expected.

In trying to discern persistent trends, Mr. Levy distinguishes between jobs that require workers to follow rules and those that require them to recognize patterns. The first—whether in manufacturing or services—are vulnerable to technology and outsourcing. The second are less vulnerable.

Consider income-tax preparation. "The tax system is based on rules . . . built into software like TaxCut and Turbo Tax," Mr. Levy and Harvard economist Richard Murnane write in

The Division of Labor, a forthcoming book. "While the preparation of complex tax returns requires expert human judgment, many other tax returns do not. . . . So it is not surprising that the preparation of routine income tax returns is beginning to move offshore." Ernst & Young LLC is sending some simple tax-return processing work to India, and a handful of U.S. companies have sprung up to help smaller accounting firms do the same.

In contrast, other jobs rely on the human ability to recognize patterns—the truck driver turning left across traffic, for instance, or the seasoned physician diagnosing an unusual disease. The doctor may rely on X-rays read by a radiologist in India or blood tests processed automatically, but diagnosing disease remains a complex human endeavor. Such jobs are proving much harder to computerize than high-tech prophets anticipated. They also are much harder to supervise from afar and thus more resistant to outsourcing abroad.

In any economy, wages for workers in high demand rise and wages for others lag or even fall.

Community colleges, publicly funded two-year colleges, excel at sniffing out jobs for which local employers are hiring—and then training for them. "Some of this stuff isn't very scientific. It's just paying attention," says Andrew Scibelli, president of Springfield Technical Community College. "When my former wife was having our child 15 years ago and had an ultrasound, I was talking to the sonographer and asked where she got her training. 'I didn't. I'm an X-ray tech. The doctors and the folks who make the equipment showed me how to do this,' she said." Mr. Scibelli went back to his office and asked his staff to look into a training program, talked to local employers, got the OK of the state bureaucracy and started a program.

Today, the program, started in 1994, draws more than 100 applicants each semester but accepts only 10, most of whom take about three years to complete the prerequisites, the coursework required for certification and clinical rotations. Graduates start at between $20 and $28 an hour.

These days community colleges are baffled by conflicting forecasts about the job outlook. "There is an incredible angst about the jobless recovery and yet there's no change in the forecast that 10 years out there will be this incredible skills shortage," says Albert Lorenzo, president of Macomb Community College outside Detroit. "All of us are trying to reconcile this."

One unpleasant possibility, acknowledged even by those firm in the trade-is-good camp, is that jobs will proliferate at both ends of the barbell—and fewer in the middle. The result would be an ever-wider gap between well-paying jobs and poorly paid jobs. That, too, has happened before, as recently as the 1980s when unionized skilled manufacturing jobs evaporated.

The overall pace of wage increases in the U.S. generally tracks growth in productivity, the amount of goods and services produced for each hour of work. But in any economy, wages for workers in high demand rise and wages for others lag or even fall.

Will technology, trade and outsourcing further widen the wage gap between the best- and worst-paid workers? Right now, the economic winds seem to be blowing that way.

For the past couple of decades, the forces of economic change have favored workers with education and skills. Though unemployment among college graduates has risen lately, the jobless rate among workers with a four-year college degree remains only 3%, well below 5.5% for high-school graduates and 8.5% for high-school dropouts.

Not every American worker whose job is now threatened is going to become a high-level software architect. What if there are only a handful of safe jobs like that left? Will everyone else's wages relentlessly fall until they meet those of Indians and Chinese in some new global equilibrium?

Beginning in the 1980s and extending into the 1990s, demand for educated workers grew far faster than the increased supply, pushing their wages far above those of lesser-skilled workers. Wages of men over age 25 with a four-year college degree are now typically 41% higher than wages of similar men with a high-school diploma, according to an analysis of government data by the Economic Policy Institute, a Washington think tank. Twenty-five years ago, the differential was just 21%. For women, the premium for a college diploma has grown to 46% from 25%.

In the late 1990s boom, wages at the very top continued to climb faster than everyone else's. But wages at the bottom moved closer to the middle class, pushed up by an unemployment rate so low that "help wanted" became the universal slogan of American businesses and by increases in the minimum wage. When the economy deteriorated in 2000 and unemployment rose, wages at the bottom fell while wages at the very top kept climbing. The premium employers pay for a college diploma remains high, though it hasn't grown lately.

The long-term solution is to spur upward mobility by getting more Americans a good education including access to college.

Will technology, trade and outsourcing further widen the wage gap between the best- and worst-paid workers?

Right now, the economic winds seem to be blowing that way. "America's long-term problem isn't too few jobs," Robert

Reich, the former Clinton administration labor secretary now at Brandeis University, wrote in a *Wall Street Journal* opinion article [in December 2003]. "It's the widening income gap. The long-term solution is to spur upward mobility by getting more Americans a good education including access to college. There will be plenty of good jobs to go around. But too few of our citizens are being prepared for them."

Without a major change in policy, such as an increase in the minimum wage or restraints on immigration, or a seismic shift in the economy, such as a surge in unions or limits on imports, the economic forces widening the gap between wages of winners and losers appear strong.

A lot depends on what happens to the latest victims of change, the white-collar analogs of the steelworkers, auto workers and other blue-collar workers pushed aside by trade and technology in the 1980s and 1990s. Some were forced to compete for poorly paid jobs with unskilled workers, including recent immigrants, pushing wages at the bottom down. Others, often with government aid, got skills needed to move up a notch.

"Rather than thinking of a career ladder," says Mr. Lorenzo, the Michigan community-college president, "we've started to refer to it as rock climbing. It's no longer a rung-by-rung clear linear progression." Some auto mechanics never mastered the repair of cars as manufacturers stuffed them with computer chips; others learned how to diagnose the computerized auto engine as well as the faulty fuel pump and prospered.

Today, the sophistication of computers and spread of overseas outsourcing threaten many of the jobs that replaced old factory jobs.

So there is another fork in the road. The low road takes these middle-skilled workers into competition for jobs washing, baby-sitting, serving and nursing the elite educated well-paid classes—pushing down wages at the bottom. The high road takes them to jobs more skilled than those they lost, the jobs that Chinese and Indians may do someday, but not yet.

Those who bet on the high road inevitably call for better educating American workers so they have skills to stay one step ahead of jobs that computers and foreign workers do. It is clear that to be a successful middle-skilled worker in the U.S. takes increasingly more schooling.

But education is a slow escalator. Harvard University President Lawrence Summers calls it "the ultimate act of faith in the future."

The gap between those with well-paying and poorly paid jobs is certain to grow.

"There are two kinds of lies that politicians tell about outsourcing," says Mr. Levy, the MIT economist. "One is that we can turn it all back. But even if you cut off all trade, technology can do the same things to workers. The other is that education is all that matters. That's true, of course, but only in the long run."

In the time spans over which economic progress is best measured—in generations—educating U.S. workers is the most appealing remedy for an economy that regularly pushes workers out of jobs they were trained to do. Without better elementary and high schools, wider access to college and more training of mature workers, the gap between those with well-paying and poorly paid jobs is certain to grow.

Over the next five or 10 years, though, better high schools, more college-student aid and more pervasive workplace training don't seem sufficient to stop outsourcing, trade, improving technology and relentless cost-cutting from widening that gap.

Greater Opportunities for the Rich Widen the Wage Gap

Mortimer B. Zuckerman

Mortimer B. Zuckerman is the chairman and editor in chief of U.S. News & World Report *and is the publisher of the* New York Daily News.

Americans remain optimistic that it is possible the American dream has not receded entirely into the mists of history. We still have faith in it because, as a people, we are natural optimists. The hard reality, however, is that it is no longer possible for more than a very small minority to start out poor, work hard, and become well off. Our fabled equal-opportunity society is in hostage to a gathering of circumstances we must address with urgency, for the sake of social justice, but also to obtain the greatest benefits from the talents of our fellow citizens and maintain a cohesive community.

The Growing Wage Gap

The generation that emerged from World War II enjoyed income growth fairly evenly spread throughout our entire population. The past 25 years tell an utterly different story. Median family incomes have risen by less than 1 percent a year—for a total of 18 percent overall—but median incomes for the top 1 percent have gone up more than 10 times faster—by an astounding 200 percent! As a nation, America has experienced extraordinary growth. From 1980 to 2004, our gross domestic product rose by almost two thirds, but when you factor in inflation, the wages of the typical earner actually fell—not a lot, but compare that with the top American earners, and the widening gap between the richest and poorest Americans becomes starkly clear: Among the top 20 percent of American earners, real incomes increased 59 percent.

And there's no sign the trend is moderating. [In 2006] the top 10 percent of wager earners are projected to receive 45 percent of all household cash income, up from 40.6 percent in 2000. And what about the average family in the 80 percent of the workforce who make up our rank and file? Incomes are actually slightly lower, after adjusting for inflation, than they were [in 2002]. This means that those Americans have effectively taken a pay cut since 2002, even as the economy has been growing by over 3 percent a year. Sadly, this isn't—or shouldn't be—terribly surprising: Except for a few years in the late 1990s, the hourly pay of most workers has done no better than inflation for the past 30 years.

Our tax system has become much less progressive, enabling families in the top decile to benefit, and especially the top within the top.

Translate these graphs going in opposite directions, and we have a picture of two highly divergent societies. Today, in fact, we have slipped back to the excesses of the notorious Gilded Age and beyond. Making matters worse, the gap between the ostentatious new rich and the rest of America is growing fast. Twenty-five years ago, the top fifth of all American households' post-tax incomes were 6.7 times those of the bottom fifth. Today, that ratio has jumped to 9.8 times— nearly a 50 percent increase. The result? More and more American workers are in danger of slipping into outright poverty. Not only were 37 million Americans living below the poverty line in 2004, but an additional 54 million were the "near poor," who live between the poverty line, earning annual incomes of roughly $19,000, and double the poverty line. Between 1982 and 2004, median earnings of fully employed men grew by only 2.7 percent. That's just about as close as you can get to absolute stagnation over a span of 22 years.

Optimists (or politicians intent on painting a rosy picture of the economy) will point you to the statistics on median family income. Don't be fooled. While the numbers show incomes up, from $43,913 to $54,061, a 23 percent growth in real terms, the growth has been due almost entirely to the fact that more and more wives have gone out to find jobs to make ends meet.

Stratification

We can now see clearly that there is no silver lining to any of these gathering clouds. If we look at net worth, as distinct from income, the growing inequality is equally manifest. Some 85 percent of the nation's wealth now resides in the hands of the richest 15 percent of American families. The bottom 50 percent of families, on the other hand, claim only 2.5 percent of household net worth. In the most recent three-year study of median family net worth, covering 2002 to 2004, the growth was virtually zero—much lower than in the previous couple of three-year periods studied. The average net worth of the richest 10 percent of American families rose to $861,000 [in 2005], a 6.5 percent increase over 2001. What happened to the typical family in the bottom 25 percent? Net worth actually fell, by 1.5 percent.

What's Going On?

First, our tax system has become much less progressive, enabling families in the top decile to benefit, and especially the top within the top. It is true that the rich have paid more taxes, but that's because their pretax earnings have taken off, up by 67 percent since 1980 compared with 12 percent for the middle fifth of society. It is here that the tax system hurts ordinary Americans most. Progressivity used to mean taxing the better-off to assist society's less fortunate. That concept has now been stood squarely on its head. Taxes for the well-to-do are lower today than they have been in 60 years. It is role reversal for Robin Hood: We are robbing the poor to enrich the rich. This is not to say that the rich aren't entitled to the fruits of their hard work, talent, risk-taking, and innovation, but the rewards for high achievers shouldn't be inconsistent with an economy that helps the average American family. And certainly the government shouldn't be exacerbating the differences in income between the rich and the nonrich. All of us have the potential to earn a comfortable living in a safe environment under the protection of our armed forces, the police, the FBI, and our firefighters. That's certainly not true of a lot of places in the world, so it's not inappropriate that our tax system should be reasonably progressive.

Why has this profound shift in incomes taken place? Is it because of foreign competition from lower-paid foreign workers or lower-paid immigrant workers, or because of the personal computer that made junior clerical workers less valuable?

Upward socioeconomic mobility is often determined by family behavior, which includes finishing an education, getting and staying married, and finding and holding a good job.

Well, the primary reason is that over the past 25 years, globalization and technology have increased the rewards for intellectual skills, vastly increasing the value of a college degree. Education and family background are replacing the old barriers of class based on race and gender. The income gap between college graduates and those without university degrees doubled between 1979 and 1997. In the 1930s and 1940s, only half of all American chief executives had college degrees. Now virtually all do, and three quarters of them also hold advanced degrees, such as an M.B.A.

The stratification in American incomes is a reflection of the stratification in education. In an era when a four-year degree has become the ultimate ticket to middle-class security and prosperity, those who have a university degree are the most likely to move out of the income bracket from which they started. Education, however, is no longer the giant escalator moving everyone inexorably upward. America's preeminence as an industrial economy in the latter part of the 19th century and the early part of the 20th was built on mass secondary education. College education, stimulated by the GI Bill after World War II, did the same for America from the 1950s on. This is beginning to change at two levels, however. At the secondary level, American education is financed largely by local property taxes so that wealthy suburbs can afford superior schools, a reverse of the days when the best public schools were in the cities. In addition, the cost of a university education has soared. An Ivy League education is out of the reach of most middle-class and poorer students. State universities, which provide a college education for 80 percent of American college graduates, have been constrained by state budget cuts over the past five years, leading to increased fees in state colleges and squeezing out students from poor and low-income families. A student from the top income quartile is six times as likely to enter the workforce with a bachelor's degree as someone from the bottom quartile: 46 percent of 24-year-olds in the top quartile earned a bachelor's degree, compared with just 8 percent from the bottom income quartile—a disparity that, believe it or not, is even worse at our most elite universities. But how could it be otherwise when tuitions at four-year colleges have more than doubled, in real terms, since 1980, reinforcing the educational gaps created by class and race, which have regressed to where they were 30 years ago?

Human Capital

The widening gap in educational opportunity is aggravated by the fact that upward socioeconomic mobility is often determined by family behavior, which includes finishing an education, getting and staying married, and finding and holding a good job. College-educated women tend to postpone children for their careers. But at the lowest income levels, more women have children younger, more have them out of wedlock, and more are without a job—whereas college graduates tend to marry other college graduates and typically enjoy the benefits of two good incomes, plus their educations.

Human capital, then, is critical. Income inequality is driven, at least in part, by human inequality, which is why we must now focus intensively on building human capital. Development of the brain function is affected by the number of words children hear from their parents, and the children of college-educated professionals hear roughly twice as many words as children of working-class parents and about three times as many as the children of welfare parents, limiting the ability of those children to develop the necessary brain function while providing dramatic advantages to the children of educated parents that continue to accumulate all along the trajectory of their academic accomplishment. That's why it is so necessary that governors and state legislators begin thinking about creating and enhancing preschool programs, because the earlier one starts learning, the better one continues to learn later on in life.

Americans still retain that great sense of optimism that derives from our faith in social mobility. To a limited extent, the concept still works. Despite the fact that very few from the bottom of society get college degrees, the majority of those who begin at the bottom still manage to climb at least one tier up the income scale, while about a third move up two or more tiers. But we must make climbing the ladder of success a reality for more and more Americans, and begin reducing the gap between the rungs. This means that governments, at all levels, must give more of a helping hand to poorer qualified college students, expand preschool education, and develop a tax system that no longer turns the American dream into an American nightmare.

Stagnant Incomes and the Rising Cost of Living Have Widened the Rich-Poor Wage Gap

Suzanne Crowell

Suzanne Crowell is a writer for the National Council of Jewish Women (NCJW). She has been a civil rights policy analyst for the U.S. Commission on Civil Rights and the U.S. Department of Housing and Urban Development.

Middle-class families once took financial stability for granted. They weren't rich, but they were comfortable. In 2007, they walk a financial tightrope, despite two incomes. They aren't going hungry, but they are struggling to keep afloat in the face of stagnant wages and sky-rocketing housing, medical, and education costs. Our nation needs the middle class. . . .

Let's say you're one half of a couple heading up a middle-class family with two or three kids in 1960. You have a reasonable expectation of owning your own home, having adequate health insurance, sending your kids to a four-year college, and taking the occasional vacation—all on one income.

Fast forward to the present, and now you are both working, earning more than ever, but feeling a lot less prosperous than you would have a generation or two ago. In fact, even with two salaries you worry constantly that the delicate financial balance of your life will topple with the next unexpected turn of events: a prolonged illness, a job loss, a parent with Alzheimer's.

You might be facing bankruptcy over your inability to pay some medical bills because your insurance was inadequate,

Suzanne Crowell, "Bridging the Economic Gap," *NCJW Journal*, vol. 30, summer 2007, pp. 13–16. Reproduced by permission.

too expensive, or simply unavailable to you once you got sick. Maybe you took out an adjustable-rate mortgage, thinking your jobs were stable and that your income would increase in real terms, like it used to, and it didn't. Maybe you had to trade up to a more expensive suburb where the public schools are better. Maybe you have sticker shock at the cost of college, more important than ever for your children's future. And because you both need to work, you now also need child care and two cars. And you may have to reinvent yourself with more education and job training to stay employed while your job gets shipped overseas or reassigned to a younger, cheaper worker. And when you retire you can no longer look forward to a traditional employer-paid pension plan.

What Happened?

Growing inequality and stagnant incomes for the majority of Americans have become recurring themes in critiques of America's economic well-being. The top 1 percent of Americans with incomes in 2005 of more than $348,000 now account for the largest share of the national income since 1928, according to the most recent available data. About 1 percent of Americans now own 40 percent of the nation's wealth, while the federal minimum wage is worth less than one-third what it was. While total personal income rose 9 percent in 2005, the individual incomes of more than 90 percent of Americans actually fell.

These two extremes—those earning $348,000 a year versus those earning the minimum wage—span a very broad range of people. Those at the bottom of this range arguably suffer most when government policies promote a skewed distribution of income and wealth while strangling safety net programs intended to prevent destitution. But the middle class is also being [squeezed financially] and things once taken for granted, like sending the kids to [college] and [having easy] access to health insurance, are no longer assumed.

President George W. Bush himself acknowledged the reality of the economic divide in a January 2007 speech.... "The fact is that income inequality is real," he said. "It's been rising for more than 25 years. And the question is whether we respond to the income inequality we see with policies that help lift people up, or tear others down." Using his criteria, where is federal policy headed? What should it be?

Federal policy is failing to move the poor out of poverty and failing to keep the middle class from sliding into economic insecurity.

In their book, *The Two-Income Trap*, Elizabeth Warren and Amelia Warren Tyagi argue that fixed costs—health care, child care, housing in a neighborhood with good schools—are rising and that two-income families today actually have less discretionary money left over than typical single-earner families did a generation ago. While some posit that the middle class spends more on unnecessary consumer goods, Warren and Tyagi say the pile of extra-cheap T-shirts replace the more expensive Sunday-best clothes middle-class children used to have in their closets. In fact, they say, in 2000 American families spent 21 percent less on clothing, 22 percent less on food, 44 percent less on major appliances, and only $170 more on the family vacation than families did in 1972–1973, according to the US Bureau of Labor.

Federal policy is failing to move the poor out of poverty and failing to keep the middle class from sliding into economic insecurity. Since the 1980s, federal budget cuts have been accompanied by assertions that the "safety net" for the poor will remain unscathed. The poor do have access to programs essential to mitigate the impact of poverty, but the programs are at best holding actions. Even these are now under attack to pay for the war in Iraq and tax cuts for the wealthy. Unfortunately, defending such programs often diverts the energy needed to devise new approaches to moving people out of poverty by increasing their earnings.

Wage Gap Solutions

A variety of strategies—public and private—to promote upward mobility could reduce poverty if they were applied on a broad scale. Increasing the minimum wage and strengthening wage and hour enforcement; expanding access to flexible leave and work schedules; encouraging employers to offer housing, child care, and transportation assistance; and tying public support for economic development to progressive employment policies, among other measures, would increase income by upgrading jobs and removing barriers to labor force participation.

In the meantime, it could be argued that middle- and working-class families stressed by stagnant incomes and rising costs for health insurance, child care, education beyond K–12, energy, and housing are in need of their own safety net to simply maintain the gains they have made or inherited from the work of their parents. Their parents' generation got an enormous boost from New Deal programs like Social Security and the benefits that came with the right to organize into unions. Post–World War II veterans programs, like those helping veterans attend college and borrow money to buy a house, lifted millions into the middle class. (It should be noted that the exclusion of blacks from many of these programs still contributes to the racial disparity in wealth and income.)

Repairing the holes in our social fabric that leave the poor without hope is urgent. But both the middle class and the poor need access to programs that deal with today's realities—affordable universal health care, affordable college tuition, assistance with child care, retraining when jobs are exported or rendered obsolete, and an equitable tax system to fund the public good. Such programs would make raising children and ensuring an adequate retirement for their parents less of a high-wire act for that 90 percent of Americans stuck with stagnant incomes.

CHAPTER 3

Is the Wage Gap Between the Races Due to Discrimination?

Chapter Preface

In 2006, nearly 120,000 workers across the country were either employed as day laborers or actively seeking employment in this informal and almost entirely unregulated sector each day, according to UCLA's Center for the Study of Urban Poverty. Day laborers seek employment by gathering at gas stations, busy intersections, parks, and other public places, offering to perform work on a day-to-day basis with no promise that more work will be available in the future. The majority of day laborers are Hispanic males, and 75 percent are undocumented immigrants, according to the UCLA center. The low wages paid to day laborers contributes to the wage gap between Hispanic males and other groups. Industries such as agriculture, textile manufacturing, food processing, and construction have relied on the immigrant workforce for decades, and the demand has not gone away.

Employers of day laborers frequently disregard U.S labor laws and worker rights, which leaves such workers vulnerable to unfair employment practices, including wage discrimination. It is not uncommon for day laborers to experience wage theft, which occurs when employers refuse to pay the agreed-upon wage or require the laborer to work more hours than originally agreed upon. Although federal labor laws apply to all employees, regardless of immigration status, day laborers are reluctant to report unfair employment practices due to fear of being deported. The majority of day laborers fall into the "working poor" category and earn less than fifteen thousand dollars a year, according to the UCLA center. Although day laborers experience frequent hardships, they continue on with the hope of someday obtaining a traditional job that is stable and better paying.

In recent years, city leaders, religious organizations, and other groups have established designated formal day laborer sites in their communities. The purpose of the sites is to provide a space for the workers to assemble, a system for job seekers and employers to connect, and to set minimum wages. However, critics argue that such sites increase illegal immigration and displace legal workers who would otherwise perform the work at a reasonable rate. Supporters of the sites, such as Siobhan McGrath, a member of the New York Day Labor Coalition, argue that the sites provide a safe place for day laborers to address discrimination and unfair employment practices. UCLA's Center for the Study of Urban Poverty estimates that approximately 80 percent of day laborer sites continue to be informal locations such as gas stations, busy intersections, parks, and other public places.

Day laborers are paid poorly because the majority of them are illegal immigrants lacking visas and work permits. As employers in the United States experience growing cost pressures, they turn to hiring undocumented workers at low wage rates. To further complicate matters, the majority of day laborers also lack education, English language proficiency, and job skills. In 2006, UCLA's Center for the Study of Urban Poverty revealed that 6 percent of day laborers have no formal education, 22 percent have five years or less of schooling, 30 percent have six to eight years of schooling, and only 42 percent have nine or more years of schooling. The low wages paid to day laborers also contribute to the wage gap between Hispanics and other races.

For the most part, day laborers depend on low-paying jobs that require physical labor, such as construction, gardening, and painting. Due to the changing economy, working in manufacturing is no longer an option even for legal workers. Plant closings and mass layoffs contribute to the growing number of Hispanics turning to day labor. Working as a day laborer helps many supplement their income while they seek other employment opportunities. For others, it is a way to obtain a first job in America. Although working as a day laborer appears to be a rough way of life, many Hispanics see it as a way to get ahead.

The majority of day laborers are in dire need of employment to care for their families. Regardless of their legal status, day laborers represent a significant component of the workforce, and thus, the economy. Day laborer critics believe day laborers accepting low-paying jobs without benefits result in the widening wage gap between the races. The viewpoints in the following chapter further explore race and wage discrimination.

Minorities Earn Less than White Males Because of Discrimination

Knight Ridder/Tribune Business News

Knight Ridder/Tribune Business News provides same-day, full-text business and related news from twenty-eight Knight Ridder publications, four Tribune Company newspapers, and more than fifty affiliated papers.

Company offices may be staffed by a growing number of blacks, Hispanics, and Asians of both genders these days, but increasing diversity isn't adding up to equal pay for workers in New Jersey.

An analysis by the [*Hackensack* (NJ)] *Record* of recent U.S. Census data for the Garden State shows that among college graduates with full-time jobs, wide gaps in pay persist between white males and every other group. In some cases the gaps are getting wider.

Facing a host of factors, including more than just racial and gender bias, women and minority men make only 54 to 81 cents for every dollar earned by their white male counterparts. The analysis found that the median full-time salary for white, college-educated men living in New Jersey in 1999 was $70,000, compared with $38,000 to $56,600 for other groups.

Although women narrowed the gap in the 1990s, minority men actually lost ground: the typical salary for white men grew over the decade by more than $21,000, compared with a gain of $13,000 to $15,000 for black, Asian, and Hispanic men.

Even Asian women, the group whose median salary rose the fastest, still earn only 71 cents for every dollar earned by white men.

Familiar barriers keeping minorities from advancing, experts say, include traditional corporate structures that don't recognize an uneven playing field; the climate of secrecy about who makes what that hides wage inequities; and the "fertile Myrtle" syndrome that continues to keep women who have children on slower career tracks.

"When you take into account the impact this has not only on pay but on pensions, you realize every family in New Jersey that has a woman or minority [group member] in it working, is being penalized," says Heather Boushey, an economist with the Center for Economic and Policy Research in Washington, D.C.

Even among those in similar job categories, the gaps are wide.

The census data show, for example, that in various management jobs in New Jersey, for every dollar white men were paid in 1999, Asian men received 85 cents, black men 68 cents, and Hispanic men 78 cents. Women, whose wage disparities are narrowing somewhat along gender lines, continue to lag behind most men. For every dollar paid white men in management jobs in 1999, white women earned 69 cents, Asian women 74 cents, black women 65 cents, and Hispanic women 63 cents. A likely reason? There are still far more white males in upper-level management positions.

One of the most glaring results of the disparity comes at the highest levels of the workplace. The analysis found that 29.8 percent of white males earned at least $100,000 in 1999, compared with 12.4 percent of blacks and 7.4 percent of women.

Legal Action

Lack of advancement is one issue. Less pay for the same work is another, although rare is the New Jersey case in which minority workers have claimed they were receiving less pay for the same work as their white-male counterparts.

"It's extremely difficult and extremely expensive to take these cases to court," says P. Kay McGahen, who won a 1989 case involving unequal pay for two private-sector women. The state Supreme Court ruling in that case set precedent in New Jersey.

Racism and sexism are really entrenched in this society and it continues to hold people back.

McGahen, who quit his legal practice to become a contractor after winning *Grigoletti vs. Ortho Pharmaceuticals*, says even having that case as a road map hasn't helped much.

"Women and minorities still have a real problem trying to address wage discrimination because if they take a chance and bring suit, they risk being fired or blacklisted," she says. "Racism and sexism are really entrenched in this society and it continues to hold people back." Cindy Morrison of Madison is trying to move ahead.

She's a leasing executive who signs retail tenants into malls owned by the publicly traded Chelsea Property Group Inc. (CPG) in Roseland. Morrison is suing her bosses over unequal pay, sexual harassment, and retaliation. The single mother, who is white and college educated, has two children in college. She says she was earning $80,729 in 2001 when she learned that at least two men doing the same job, but who had slightly different titles, were paid as much as $30,000 more, plus bigger bonuses. Morrison was especially angry, she says, because she was closing more lucrative deals for CPG than her higher-paid, white-male counterparts.

"It was very distressing," says Morrison. "It's like a whole salary difference for most women." After filing suit against CPG on February 6, under the state's Law Against Discrimination, Morrison says she was promoted on March 13, given the same title as the two colleagues and a $31,647 raise, bringing her total base salary for th[e] year to $115,000. It's the same amount she says one of the men was earning two years ago, while the other got paid a base of at least $120,000.

"They make more than me today," she says. "It's still not equal pay." Despite the promotion, Morrison plans to take her claims to a mediator in an effort to get back pay and damages. Attorneys say mediation is a fairly common way to go in an effort to settle these and a growing number of other cases. But if the two sides can't agree on an outcome, Morrison can press on in court.

"I had to consider the money, the emotional stress and wonder where I would ever get hired again," Morrison says of trying to decide whether to even file suit. "But in the end, even after getting promoted, I decided in my heart that I have to follow through, especially since so many women and minorities who are hurt by these practices can't afford to."

Julie Werner, an attorney representing CPG, says the company denies Morrison's allegations. Werner says they are "factually inaccurate" and that "the fact that she was promoted had nothing to do with the fact that she was filing a lawsuit." Cases in New Jersey can be challenged under the state Law Against Discrimination, the federal Equal Pay Act of 1963, which aimed to end wage disparities for women, or under Title VII of the Civil Rights Act of 1964, which says employees cannot be discriminated against based on race, color, religion, sex, or national origin. Title VII requires people to first file a complaint with the Equal Employment Opportunity Commission.

[Latinos are] the last ones to be hired and the first to be let go and it's not because the person doesn't have the qualifications or the experience.

"Each has its difficulties," says Fort Lee employment attorney Stephen Kahn. "But the real remedies are not going to stem from lawsuits alone. Lawsuits and statutes are bridges to justice, but they're not substitutes for employers and other people taking action to address wrongs." Recognizing the problem is a first step, he and others say.

Solutions

The research shows that as a group, Asians made the most gains and Latinos the least.

"It's been a bad situation for Latino men and women for a long time," says Daniel H. Jara, president and CEO [chief executive officer] of the Hispanic Chamber of Commerce of New Jersey. "They're the last ones to be hired and the first to be let go and it's not because the person doesn't have the qualifications or the experience." Jara believes one fix is for the Latino community to "make corporations aware" of their purchasing power. He and others also say stronger legislation and changes in the way companies recognize and reward talent would help put all workers on more equal footing.

"Organizations are set up to identify talent in one model and that model has traditionally been male," says Linda Bates Parker, president and founder of Black Career Women, a national professional development group.

The model typically rewards men who temporarily leave work to serve in the military, but slows the progress of women who take time off to have children. She also believes that increasing the contact white men who run companies have with minorities could improve pay disparities along racial and ethnic lines.

"For all this to change for African-Americans and Hispanics," Bates Parker says, "the white males need greater exposure to people of diversity so that our values and differences are appreciated." John F. Robinson, president and CEO of the National Minority Business Council, says it's also worth realizing that people in power aren't eager to give it up.

"People don't give up privilege," says Robinson, whose group helps minorities start their own businesses. "We can monitor laws and bring challenges where possible, but in the final analysis, Afro-Americans might do better as entrepreneurs than in corporate life." Betty Spence says people who choose to stay within the corporate structure would benefit from having increased access to influential colleagues.

"A lot of the pay disparities are unintentional," says Spence, president of the National Association for Female Executives. "Women aren't part of informal networks. Sally's not on the golf course, but Sam is, so Sam gets the job, he's considered a 'good fit.'" Wage disparities also occur because of occupational segregation. As projects director for the state's council on Gender Parity in Labor and Education, Mary Gatta has found that jobs historically held by white men pay more.

The one place where salary gaps do not favor white men is among the youngest workforce, a phenomenon that could merely reflect everyone starting at the same point after college or could signal a true change coming in the next decade or two.

The census analysis found that for full-time employees under 30 years old, Asian men led the way with a median salary of $55,000, while white men earned about the same as Hispanic and black men. But once workers hit their 30s, white men surged ahead. The typical college-educated white man 30 to 40 years old earned $69,000, with Asian men second, at $58,500.

"Workers in various jobs tend to start out on much more equal footing," Gatta says. "But so far, a great deal of research suggests that the wage gap gets wider and wider as we age."

Minority Women Still Earn the Least Pay for the Same Work

Marianne Sullivan

Marianne Sullivan is a Women's eNews *correspondent.*

Authors of the latest annual wage report by the Institute for Women's Policy Research find a conspicuously wider gender wage gap for minority women.

"I would say that things had been stagnating over the past years in terms of women overall," said Amy Caiazza, the study's director. "What is new about the report that we find interesting is how much what kind of women you are matters. There are vast differences between race and ethnicity that had not really been covered before."

The earnings ratio between men and women employed year round and full time in 2002 was 76.2 percent, that is, women earned 76.2 cents for every dollar men earned. When women of color were compared to white men, however, the gap became larger. African American women earn just 63 cents and Hispanic women earn only 53 cents for each dollar that white men earn. Asian American women were the highest paid group of all women and had the narrowest wage gap, 75 cents. The gap for white women was found to be 70 cents.

Wage gaps also exist within minority men and women. For instance, in 1999, white women made an average of $30,900 compared with white men, who made on average $44,200. African American women, again, on average, made $26,600 versus $33,100 earned by African American men.

Caiazza says the study will help to create a clearer picture of differences that exist among categories of women, which will be important for policy makers as they seek to eradicate the root causes of the wage gap.

"We hope that the research will help people make better policies," Caiazza said. "The study clearly says that 'one size does not fit all' and that there are different problems and different levels of problems that have to be taken into consideration. It clearly says that gender is a factor but race is also a factor."

Stubborn Wage Gap

The report confirms a stubborn gender-wage gap more than 40 years after passage of the Equal Pay Act. Women, it finds, in addition to experiencing a wage gap, also are less likely to own a business and work in highly paid jobs, such as those in science or technology, or at top levels of business.

On [the day] the report appeared, news broke that a panel of arbitrators had found that Merrill Lynch and Company, the nation's biggest brokerage firm, discriminated against women who worked as stockbrokers. The panel made the judgment while it awarded $2.2 million to a Merrill Lynch stockbroker. This was the first legal ruling to find that a Wall Street firm had engaged in systematic discrimination.

Women who had worked as brokers at Merrill Lynch and Smith Barney, a unit of Citigroup, filed mass claims of sex discrimination in the late 1990s. They contended that the firms continued to favor men and pay them more.

If the gap continues narrowing at the rate it did between 1989 and 2002, women would not achieve wage parity for more than 50 years. This figure was calculated using data from the Institute of Women's Policy Research and the Urban Institute.

The data in the report comes from several sources, including the 2000 Census and the 2002 and 2003 Current Population Survey.

Released on Equal Pay Day

The report was released in conjunction with "Equal Pay Day," a national event sponsored by various women's organizations, including the National Committee on Pay Equity, to publicize the goal of ending wage discrimination against women and people of color.

Many women's groups use the report, Women's Economic Status in the States: Wide Disparities by Race, Ethnicity and Region, to spread the word that, even as women make progress, the gap in wages will likely take years to eradicate.

The National Women's Law Center, in a press release, called for stronger enforcement of the Equal Pay Act by enacting provisions of the Paycheck Fairness Act, now incorporated into the omnibus Civil Rights Act of 2004.

Female-dominated and jobs dominated by people of color are undervalued and underpaid

---

The Paycheck Fairness Act would ensure effective remedies for wage discrimination and make it easier to sue on behalf of groups of women.

The Washington advocacy group also urged passage of the Fair Pay Act, which would address the problem of paying lower wages in fields dominated by women and people of color.

"One of the problems that women and people of color face in the work force is that female-dominated and jobs dominated by people of color are undervalued and underpaid," said Deborah Chalfie, senior counsel of the National Women's Law Center. "That is a feature of the labor market that is clearly an impediment to pay equity. We believe that these two legislative measures would be two huge steps in addressing some of the structural factors that contribute to pay inequity as well as addressing them in a procedural area."

Michele Leber has been fighting this battle both personally and as the chair of the National Committee on Pay Equity for more than 20 years. She and other librarians in Fairfax County, Va., sued the county to receive wages in line with other salaries paid by the county.

"My field is predominately female and studies have shown that the higher the percentage of women in a field, the lower the salary," Leber said. The case was dismissed by the Equal Employment Opportunity Commission, which said the case did not fall under its jurisdiction.

"We don't expect them to get far in a Republican congress," said Leber, referring to current attempts to pass legislation guaranteeing equal wages, "and even though these bills were introduced years ago, we expect them to take years more to get passed."

Minorities Earn Less than Whites Because of Racial Inequalities

Tim Wise

Tim Wise is the author of two recently published books: White Like Me: Reflections on Race from a Privileged Son *and* Affirmative Action: Racial Preference in Black and White.

Whenever I write an article about racism, or give a speech concerning the ongoing reality of discrimination in the labor market, I am assailed by those who refuse to believe what virtually any study done in the past two decades confirms: namely, that people of color are not seeing things, nor crazy when they suggest that racial bias is very much a modern-day phenomenon.

These assaults typically arrive in my e-mail inbox, within hours of an article going out over the web, as if pre-prepared long before, and as if their authors were simply waiting for an opportunity to pick an electronic fight.

Sometimes their retorts are little more than racist rants about how blacks and Latinos are lazy, or how American Indians are all drunk. But oftentimes the denial comes wrapped in far more sophisticated garb than that, occasionally bordering on the scholarly, in fact.

Experience and Qualifications

While some of the conservatives who regale me with their rationalizations for racial inequality manage to quote a gaggle of right wing "experts" to help make their case, the claims they forward are hardly the stronger for it.

Tim Wise, "Excuses, Excuses: How the Right Rationalizes Racial Inequality in America (Part One)," *The Black Commentator*, May 5, 2005. www.blackcommentator.com/137/ 137_wise_1.html. Reproduced by permission of the publisher and the author.

For example, the argument that racial wage gaps merely reflect different levels of experience and qualifications between whites and blacks is simply untenable, when one examines the data.

Fact is, earnings gaps persist at all levels of education. According to Census data, whites with high school diplomas, college degrees or Master's Degrees all earn approximately twenty percent more than their black counterparts. Even more striking, whites with professional degrees (such as medicine or law) earn, on average, thirty-one percent more than similar blacks and fifty-two percent more than similar Latinos.

Even when levels of work experience are the same between blacks and whites, the racial wage gap remains between 10–20 percent.

Test scores and other academic achievement differences can account for no more than three percent of the wage gaps between whites and blacks.

Looking at whites and blacks of similar age, doing the same work, earnings gaps remain significant. Among 25–34 year olds, white lawyers, computer programmers, and carpenters earn, on average, about one-fourth more than comparable blacks; white doctors and accountants earn, on average, one-third more than comparable blacks; and even white janitors earn sixteen percent more, on average, than comparable blacks.

Although these gaps do not necessarily reflect overt discrimination by employers—in fact, they mostly reflect the segmented labor market, whereby whites have greater access to more lucrative clients and companies—the effect is the same: whites continue to receive advantages in the labor market over equally qualified blacks.

And contrary to the claims of some, differences in black and white wages are not the result of different cognitive abilities or IQ scores. The results of over thirty studies confirm that test scores and other academic achievement differences can account for no more than three percent of the wage gaps between whites and blacks.

Age

The two most common excuses for racial wage inequity are age and geography: excuses popularized by black conservatives like [syndicated columnist] Thomas Sowell, and repeated ad infinitum by white reactionaries like [scholars] Abigail and Stephen Thernstrom.

Since blacks are, on average, younger than whites they will earn less, so the argument goes; and since blacks disproportionately live in the South—a lower-wage region of the country—they will earn less, even if there were no racism operating in labor markets.

Black men with college degrees earn, on average, 20–25 percent less than comparable white men, even when they are the same age.

Regarding age, though the median age among whites is about nine years older than the median for blacks, and although persons who are older typically earn more than those who are younger, this fact does not explain differences between white and black earnings, and even to the extent it is a factor, it cannot be separated from the issue of racism.

First, even when whites and blacks of comparable age are compared, wage gaps remain substantial. Black men with college degrees earn, on average, 20–25 percent less than comparable white men, even when they are the same age.

White families headed by persons of every age group are far better off than comparable blacks, and indeed a black family headed by a 45–54 year old is 3.5 times more likely to be poor than a comparable white family, and twenty percent more likely to be poor than a white family headed by someone who is twenty years younger!

Longer Life Expectancy

Secondly, the older median age for whites is due to a larger number of elderly citizens, which is the result of longer life expectancy. But of course, life expectancy itself is related to racism, so age gaps between whites and blacks hardly qualify as an independent variable to explain income inequality.

As a number of studies have documented, blacks routinely have less access to high-quality health care, and also suffer from discriminatory treatment at the hands of doctors. Even when health care is available, doctors are less likely to order a full range of diagnostic tests and treatments for black patients than for whites, even when these patients' finances and insurance coverage are comparable to their white counterparts.

Even when comparing blacks and whites of comparable age, sex, severity of disease, geographic location, and other factors that could influence the quality of medical treatment, blacks are sixty percent less likely to receive a coronary angioplasty or bypass surgery to relieve a serious heart condition.

As one study found, doctors presented with identical patient histories and symptoms overwhelmingly refer whites for more advanced treatment. According to the study, which presented doctors with videotaped patient interviews (actually actors trained to pose as patients with identical medical histories and symptoms), doctors were far less likely to refer black women for aggressive treatment of cardiac symptoms than white women.

When asked to give their impression of the actors (whom they believed to be real patients), doctors routinely said they perceived the black "patients" as less intelligent, less likely to follow doctor's recommendations and thus cooperate with a treatment regimen, and more likely to miss appointments:

this, despite the fact that the actors had made identical comments and had presented identical symptoms.

So, if whites have a longer life expectancy, and if this is due in part to racially disparate provision of health care, it is absurd to claim that the younger average age of the black community explains racial earnings gaps, independent of racism, since the age gaps and racism are intimately related.

Even racism experienced outside the realm of health care is correlated with negative health outcomes. After all, the biggest killer of African Americans is high blood pressure leading to stroke, heart disease and kidney failure; and high blood pressure has been shown to be associated with experiences with racism.

More Black Youths

Additionally, there is a significant reason why median ages for whites and blacks, despite their disparity, would have virtually no actual impact on median wages for either group, and thus would be incapable of explaining racial earnings gaps: namely, the younger median age for blacks is caused by a disproportionate number of youth in the black community relative to whites. But neither the elderly whites who skew white average ages upward, nor black youth who skew black average ages downward, have an effect on median earnings for either group. This should be obvious since neither white elderly or black children are generally in the labor force, and thus are incapable of affecting the earnings of those between the ages of 15–65 who are.

The only real issue of importance in terms of relative white or black ages, and how those might affect earnings, is the relative ages of whites and blacks who are actually in the labor force, or potential labor force, which will generally mean those between 15–65.

If anything, white workers are probably a bit younger on average than black workers, for two reasons. First, white teens are more likely to be working or looking for work thanks to greater job opportunities. Indeed, there is a persistent 15–20 percentage point gap between white and black teen unemployment rates. While whites are only sixty-five percent of persons 15–17, they are seventy-six percent of such persons with a job (thereby affecting wage rates). Likewise, blacks are fifteen percent of 15–17 year olds, but less than eight percent of such persons with a job.

Secondly, blacks are more likely to work longer into their older years, thanks to having less accumulated capital and thus being unable to retire as early as whites. So, if anything, the median age of those in the workforce would likely be higher for blacks than whites, which means that using conservative logic, the older average black workforce should earn more than its younger white counterpart.

According to Census data, 66.5 percent of whites and sixty-six percent of blacks are between the ages of 15–64: the years of typical labor market eligibility; sixteen percent of whites and sixteen percent of blacks are 35–44 and fifteen percent of whites and a little more than twelve percent of blacks are 45–54, the peak earning years for those in the American labor market.

In other words, the median age differences for the cohorts whose potential presence in the labor market might actually affect wages are not capable of explaining the substantial wage differentials between blacks and whites.

Geography

Finally, some dismiss claims of discrimination as central to the earnings gap, by claiming that disparities are largely a function of geography. In other words, because blacks are concentrated in the South and because the South is a lower-wage region, naturally blacks will have lower median earnings.

But where blacks live is hardly a variable that is independent of racism: after all, blacks are heavily concentrated in the

South due to a history of slavery and sharecropping that was disproportionately concentrated in the Southern states. As such, to whatever extent geography plays a role in lower black wages, it is impossible to disentangle this reality from the history of racial oppression.

Even if one controls for location of residence and only compares like families, racial disparities remain.

Secondly, although there are earnings differences between families living in different regions, these differences are far smaller than the observed racial gaps. The region with the least blacks, for example, only outstrips the South in terms of median earnings by about a thousand dollars annually.

This is far below the typical racial gap between white and black families, which is over $15,000 a year.

In truth, black median incomes in every region are lower than median incomes for whites, so that even if one controls for location of residence and only compares like families, racial disparities remain.

As a parent, I have learned how readily children will offer virtually any excuse for their own misbehaviors, some of which can be quite creative, even comical. While such prevarication can be endearing when practiced by a four year old, it becomes quite a bit less amusing when practiced by so-called social scientists out to debunk what all rational persons realize, and what all the best evidence demonstrates: namely, that racism is far from a thing of the past, and that whites continue to receive substantial privileges and preferences in the American labor market.

Low-Wage Immigrant Workers Contribute to the Racial Wage Gap

Randolph Capps, Michael E. Fix, Jeffrey S. Passel,
Jason Ost, and Dan Perez-Lopez

Randy Capps is a demographer and research associate at the Urban Institute. Michael E. Fix directs the Immigration Studies Program at the Urban Institute. Jeffrey S. Passel is a demographer and principal research associate at the Urban Institute. Jason Ost is a research assistant at the Urban Institute. Dan Perez-Lopez is a former research assistant at the Urban Institute.

During the 1990s, one out of every two new workers was an immigrant. While many immigrants speak English well and enter the United States with strong academic credentials and skills, many others do not. Like other low-skilled workers, few of these immigrants enjoy the benefits of employer-provided training programs, most of which are geared to managers or highly skilled workers. Low-wage immigrant workers have also been outside the reach of government-sponsored job training programs that concentrate on getting welfare recipients into the labor market and have often underserved persons with limited English skills.

The nation's workforce development and training policies are now being reconsidered as employers look for more ways to raise workers' skills. Further, the reauthorization of the 1998 Workforce Investment Act (WIA)—the largest source of federal funding for job training, adult basic education, and English as a second language (ESL) instruction—would give states and providers more incentives to serve limited English proficient (LEP) populations and encourage programs to combine adult education, ESL, and job-training services if proposals now on the table are adopted. The results provided here shed light on the need for policies that move in these directions.

Approach and Data

Our study examines the size of the low-wage immigrant labor force, as well as the educational attainment, English language ability, legal status, and gender of low-wage immigrant workers. The data come from the March 2002 Supplement to the Current Population Survey (CPS). We define "workers" as people ages 18 to 64 who: are in the civilian workforce; report positive wage and salary earnings for 2001; and have worked at least 25 weeks (i.e., at least some hours over the course of six months) or 700 hours (i.e., full-time equivalent for 20 weeks) during 2001. We define the workforce as broadly as possible but exclude students and other casual part-time workers. Using other definitions of the labor force does not substantially affect the overall results.

Immigrants are substantially overrepresented among workers who are paid the least and are most in need of training to improve their skills and earnings.

We define the low-wage labor force as workers earning less than 200 percent of their state's prevailing minimum wage. Data on workers earning less than the minimum wage are also included.

Immigrant Shares of the Labor Force

The share of immigrant workers has risen rapidly due to high immigration levels over the past two decades. While immigrants represent roughly 11 percent of the total U.S. population, they make up 14 percent of the U.S. labor force and 20 percent of the nation's low-wage labor force. By our definition, there were 125.3 million workers in the United States in 2002, 17.9 million of whom were foreign-born. There were 43.1 million low-wage workers, 8.6 million of whom were foreign-born. Two million immigrant workers earned less than the minimum wage.

Immigrants are substantially overrepresented among workers who are paid the least and are most in need of training to improve their skills and earnings. Nearly half (48 percent) of all immigrant workers earned less than 200 percent of the minimum wage, compared with 32 percent of native workers. The average low-wage immigrant worker earned $14,400 in 2001.

Educational Attainment

A key barrier to participation in WIA and employer-provided training programs is lack of formal schooling, as most of these programs are geared towards enrollees with at least a ninth-grade education. Eighteen percent of the immigrant labor force has less than a ninth-grade education. Another 12 percent of immigrant workers have completed the ninth grade but not high school. In all, 30 percent of immigrant workers (versus only 8 percent of native workers) have not finished high school.

Among *low-wage* immigrant workers, nearly half (45 percent) have less than a high school education and over a quarter (28 percent) have not completed the ninth grade.

Overall, 5.3 million immigrant workers do not have a high school diploma, accounting for 39 percent of all U.S. workers who have not completed high school. The 3.3 million immigrant workers who have not completed the ninth grade represent about 75 percent of all workers with so little education.

Limited English Proficiency

Almost half (46 percent) of all foreign-born workers are "limited English proficient" (LEP), according to data from Census 2000. Nearly three-quarters (73 percent) of LEP workers speak

Spanish. Much smaller shares speak other languages, led by Chinese (4 percent), Vietnamese (4 percent), and Korean (2 percent). While time in the United States and work experience reduce the share of workers who are LEP, 29 percent of workers who have been in the country for 20 years or more can still be considered LEP. In general, limited English skills are closely associated with low-wage work, but nearly two-thirds (62 percent) of low-wage immigrant workers are LEP, compared with only 2 percent of low-wage natives. The vast majority of all LEP workers—84 percent—are foreign-born.

Undocumented immigrants are more likely to lack English proficiency and a ninth-grade education.

Not surprisingly, limited English proficiency and limited education go hand in hand. Nationwide, 28 percent of the overall U.S. labor force with less than a high-school education is LEP, though almost all of these LEP workers are foreign-born. Eighty-three percent of immigrant workers with less than a ninth-grade education, and 66 percent who complete the ninth grade but not high school, are LEP. That said, 23 percent of immigrant workers with a bachelor's degree or beyond are also LEP, and 37 percent of low-wage workers with some college or a college degree are LEP.

Legal Status

Immigrants' legal status helps determine access to job-training and work-support programs. Indeed, eligibility for most government-sponsored programs is restricted to legal immigrants under federal law. Legal status is also associated with limited English language skills and low education levels: undocumented immigrants are more likely to lack English proficiency and a ninth-grade education.

Of the 17.9 million foreign-born workers in the United States, some 12.7 million are here legally. Thirty-four percent of immigrant workers are naturalized citizens, 34 percent are legal immigrants (including refugees), and 29 percent are undocumented. Compared to the workforce in general, the low-wage labor force has a higher share of undocumented immigrants and a lower share of naturalized citizens. Of the 8.6 million low-wage immigrant workers, 3.4 million (40 percent) are undocumented. Less than a quarter (23 percent) are naturalized citizens.

Gender Composition

A striking feature of the immigrant labor force is how few foreign-born women join it, compared with native women. Overall, women make up about half (48 percent) of the native workforce, but only 40 percent of the immigrant workforce. In the low-wage labor force, a clear majority (59 percent) of natives are female, compared with only 44 percent of low-wage foreign-born workers.

Gender differences are even more pronounced among undocumented workers. Only 32 percent of all undocumented workers and 37 percent of low-wage undocumented workers are women. This differential reflects very high labor-force participation among undocumented men and relatively low labor participation among undocumented women. Female immigrants—especially undocumented women—participate at lower rates because they are far more likely to be married, and because they have more children on average than native-born women. In short, undocumented men come to the U.S. mainly to work, while many undocumented women come to be with their families.

Although they have lower labor-force participation, immigrant women who do take low-wage jobs are better educated than their male counterparts. More than three-fourths (76 percent) of female low-wage immigrant workers hold at least a high school diploma, compared with 66 percent of male low-wage immigrant workers. They are also more likely to be proficient in English than foreign-born male workers: 59 versus 50 percent.

Even though immigrant women are more likely to be in the United States legally, hold high school diplomas, and speak English, their earnings trail those of immigrant men. Thirteen percent of immigrant women earn less than the minimum wage, compared with 9 percent of foreign-born men and native women. Forty percent of immigrant women earn from 100 to 200 percent of the minimum wage, compared with 36 percent of foreign-born men and 31 percent of native women. Clearly, many legally present, comparatively well-educated immigrant women in the labor force could benefit from training and other avenues to higher earnings.

Occupations

Immigrant workers represent an especially large share of the total U.S. labor force in two major occupation groups: private household services (42 percent are immigrants), and farming, forestry, and fishing (37 percent). Looking only at low-wage immigrant workers, the share is even higher (44 percent in each). Workers in these two occupations are the least well paid and the most likely to be foreign-born of all major occupational groups tracked by the Census. Even so, only 6 percent of all immigrant workers and 10 percent of low-wage immigrant workers hold jobs in these occupations.

The other occupation groups with significant shares of low-wage immigrant workers include service occupations (except protective services); precision production, crafts and repair; machine operators and assemblers; and administrative support. In those occupational categories, wages are usually higher and worker-training opportunities more plentiful.

Low-Wage Immigrant Worker Outlook

Immigrants make up one in nine U.S. residents, one in seven U.S. workers, and one in five low-wage workers. Immigrants are overrepresented among both low-wage and less educated U.S. workers. Since so many immigrants work and so many hold low-wage jobs, they could potentially benefit from post- as well as pre-employment services.

Unfortunately, most publicly funded training programs assume that participants have ninth-grade levels of literacy, numeracy, and basic English skills, and most privately funded training programs are geared to skilled workers and managers. To fill the gap, Congress should consider revamping the Workforce Investment Act, and employers should tailor their job-training programs to serve LEP populations, build language assessment capacity, and combine job training with English language, basic education, and literacy instruction.

Female workers are of particular concern. Compared to native women, fewer immigrant women participate in the labor force. Immigrant women who work are better educated and more likely to enjoy legal status than foreign-born men, but earn less than either foreign-born men or native women. Thus, raising the incomes of immigrant families requires targeting education, training, and other post-employment services toward women who work—or want to—in these families.

While immigrants dominate a few low-wage occupations—farming and private household workers—the immigrants working in those occupations represent a relatively small share of all immigrant workers. Overall, there are far more foreign-born workers in such occupations as low-skilled manufacturing and services, so expanding training opportunities in these economic sectors should help large numbers of immigrant workers.

The Racial Wage Gap Is Due to Multiple Factors

Maryland Department of Labor, Licensing, and Regulation

The Maryland Department of Labor, Licensing, and Regulation (DLLR) is committed to safeguarding and protecting Maryland citizens and supporting the economic stability of the state by providing businesses, the workforce, and the consuming public with high-quality, customer-focused regulatory and employment and training services.

Just as a wage gap can be found in earnings of men and women, a wage gap also exists among some racial and ethnic groups in America. The controversial question is why the wage gap exists—to what factors can it be attributed? Research suggests various answers—skill disparity, differences in work patterns, differences in choice of industry/occupation, economic changes, and discrimination. Each of these possibilities has different policy implications. Before any progress can be made in eliminating wage disparity between racial and ethnic groups, it must be determined which of the possibilities is responsible for the wage gap.

Education

One's level of education plays a big role in how much one earns and will earn in the future. . . .

While rates of enrollment are very similar among all groups for high school, Hispanics' and blacks' rates of high school completion are lower than those of whites and Asians. According to the U.S. Census Bureau, of all eighteen through twenty-four year olds who were included in the census in 2000, 91.8% of whites, 83.7% of blacks, 64.1% of Hispanics,

Maryland Department of Labor, Licensing, and Regulation, Appendix C: Report of the Equal Pay Commission, *Report to the Maryland State Commission on Equal Pay— Raced- Based Wage Disparities*, December 6, 2006. Reproduced by permission.

and 94.6% of Asians completed high school. A similar trend can be found for college completion. According to the Integrated Postsecondary Education Data System (IPEDS) Graduation Rate Survey published in 2003, blacks and Hispanics complete college at lower rates also. Of all people who began college in 1997, 59% of whites completed college within six years or less, while only 40% of blacks and 42% of all Hispanics that began college in 1997 completed it within the same time period. A huge gap exists also in advanced degrees. According to the U.S. Census Survey of Income and Program Participation of 2001, out of the total 16,180,000 advanced degrees held by people in America, 82.4% were held by whites, 6% were held by blacks, 3.6% were held by Hispanics, and the rest by other minorities. As the data reveals, at practically all levels of education, blacks and Hispanics have a lower level of participation and completion.

Various resources show that a greater percentage of black and Hispanic men than white and Asian men do not participate in the labor force.

Why is education so important? It has been proven in various research that level of education and earnings have a positive correlation. . . .

Wages are not only affected by the level education of the individual, but also correlate to the level of education of the individual's parents. For whites and blacks whose parents had less than a college education, whites consistently earn more than blacks. However, in a situation where the parents had some college education or more, blacks earn more than their white counterparts.

While various data demonstrate that blacks and Hispanics are less educated than whites and Asians when measuring by degrees earned, the question that remains is why an earnings gap remains for people of roughly the same level of education but of different racial or ethnic groups. One explanation is that the data available often does not control for both level of education and years of experience. Just as in comparing wages of men and women, women of all ages tended to have less work experience than men, differing work patterns of different racial and ethnic groups may have an affect on wages and earnings.

Work Patterns

Various resources show that a greater percentage of black and Hispanic men than white and Asian men do not participate in the labor force; of those people who are in the labor force, there are twice as many blacks unemployed as whites. Moreover, blacks and Hispanics tend to work fewer weeks per year and fewer hours per week, are overrepresented in temporary and on-call work, and tend to be unemployed for longer periods of time than whites.

Rates of participation in the labor market, as well as rates of employment and unemployment are one way to compare work experience among racial and ethnic groups, which could explain some of the gap in wages and earnings. . . .

The differences in number of weeks worked per year and number of hours worked per week by the different racial and ethnic groups may also reveal information about the gap in wages and earnings. According to the California labor market data, among all working men compared in 2000, blacks worked 46 weeks per year on average, while whites worked 48. In terms of hours worked per week, blacks and Hispanics worked about 41 hours per week, while whites worked 44 hours per week. This is also reflected when hourly wages are compared to annual earnings. According to "Basic Skills and the Black-White Earning Gap" by [Derek] Neal and [William R.] Johnson, black men in America earn 48% less per year than whites of the same age, even though their wages are only 24% lower. This statistic suggests that black men may be working less time overall.

Hispanics and blacks are more likely than whites to be unemployed for longer periods of time.

The type of jobs people hold can greatly affect their wages also. According to "The Big Payoff" the earnings of workers who work full time year round tend to be significantly higher than the earnings of workers who work part time or just part of the year. When compared to whites, blacks' and Hispanics' participation in non-standard work (regular part-time, temporary help agency, on-call/day labor, self employed, independent contractor) is proportional to the size of its population, and maybe even slightly low. However, in two worst areas of non-standard jobs—temporary and on-call labor, both of which tend to pay little and offer few benefits, if any, blacks and Hispanics are overrepresented. . . .

Another important factor that must be considered is whether there are differences between how long people of different racial and ethnic groups are unemployed. Hispanics and blacks are more likely than whites to be unemployed for longer periods of time. In 2000, 29% of all long-term unemployed Americans were black, 16.9%, were Hispanic, and 48.3% were white. When compared to the percentage each racial and ethnic group makes up in the total population (whites—9%, blacks—16%, and Hispanics—12%), it is clear that blacks and Hispanics are disproportionately represented among the long-term unemployed group. Moreover, when compared to the 20% that blacks made up of the total unemployed in 2000, the 29% is very high. Of all people long-term unemployed, blacks had the highest percentage of people that were unemployed for over six months at 22.7%, while whites had 17.6%, and Hispanics had 14.2%.

Choice of Industry/Occupation

Besides the differences between racial and ethnic groups in work patterns, differences can also be found in their choices of industry and occupation. According to the U.S. Census Survey of 2000, 35.6% of white men, and 44.6% of Asian men were employed in managerial, professional and related occupations, compared with 25.2% of black men and just 18% of Hispanic men. On the other hand, about 40% of black and Hispanic men held jobs in service, production, transportation, and material moving occupations, compared to 27% of white men and Asian men. A disproportionately high percentage of black and Hispanic women compared with white and Asian women held jobs with poor pay, few benefits, and little career mobility such as food preparation, cleaning, and personal care.

These statistics beg the question why people of different races end up in different occupations. One answer is obvious—differences in education; because a great percentage of blacks and Hispanics do not acquire a high school or a college degree, they work jobs in service, production, transportation, and material moving. Another reason may be the existence of so called "ethnic niches". New York City provides a broad example of ethnic niches; there, Hispanics predominantly work in construction, Asians run laundry mats and dry cleaning businesses, white men work as fire fighters, etc. While such niches can help members of the prevalent racial or ethnic group at that job obtain a job by providing training and shelter from discrimination, such jobs pay less, and can often constrain job mobility. Once an ethnic niche is created in a certain occupation or industry the desirability and availability of the job becomes limited [according to researcher Roberta Spalter-Roth].

Another difference could be simply the variation in choices made by people of different racial and ethnic groups in college. According to "Why Do Minorities Earn Less? A Study of

Wage Differentials among the Highly Educated," the index of dissimilarity indicates that 14% of Hispanic men, 20% of black men, and 31% of Asian men would need to change their major to match the distribution of majors among whites. Asians, for example, are more likely to major in engineering than any other group, while black men tend to be underrepresented in engineering and overrepresented in education. Black men also choose majors that on average have a higher fraction of women, while Asian men choose majors that have a lower fraction of women.

[One] test revealed that three-fourths of the racial wage gap for men is due to a skill disparity. For women, the test scores explained all of the wage disparity.

One other possibility that could explain why people of different racial and ethnic groups end up in different occupations, is discrimination. Rather than looking at each person's credentials like education and experience, employers look at skin color, and base their hiring decisions on racial and ethnic identities of past employees. For example, if in all the years of a company's existence the position of vice-president has been filled by a white male, it may take a long time before a woman or a minority will be hired for that position, simply because the hiring personnel may feel more comfortable giving the position to someone who is similar to other people who have held that position in the past. Thus, blacks continue to be hired for certain types of jobs in certain occupations, reinforcing existing ethnic niches.

Skill Disparity

One important factor that may shine some light on the cause of the wage gap between racial and ethnic groups is skill. While looking at the level of education has been the traditional and common way to determine one's ability level and predict future wages, recent researchers have contended that this information can be misleading because the quality of schools and intensity of education in different schools vary greatly in America. Just as age is not a valid predictor of one's level of education, the amount of schooling one has doesn't truly reveal that person's ability. In "The Role of Premarket Factors in Black-White Wage Differences" Derek Neal and William Johnson discuss a different measure of education—skill. For their research, Neal and Johnson used the scores from the Armed Forces Qualification Test (AFQT) found in the National Longitudinal Survey of Youth, to examine the black-white wage gap among workers in their late twenties (age 26–29). The AFQT is known to be a racially unbiased measure of basic skills that helps predict job performance, and is often used in military testing. The data set included a sample of individuals who were tested at ages 16–18, just before they entered the labor force full time or began their secondary education. Testing for math and reading skills, the results of the test revealed that three-fourths of the racial wage gap for men is due to a skill disparity. For women, the test scores explained all of the wage disparity. In fact, when the AFQT scores were held constant for white, black, and Hispanic women, black and Hispanic women earned more than white women. . . .

Besides the disparity that exists in cognitive skills, disparity is apparent also with non-cognitive skills such as motivation, self control, time preference, and social skills. In the CNLSY [Children of the National Longitudinal Survey of Youth], mothers were asked age-specific questions about the anti-social behavior of their children, including aggressiveness, violent behavior, cheating, lying, disobedience, peer conflicts, and social withdrawal. The results showed that by age 5 and 6, the average black is roughly 10 percentile points above the average white (the higher the score, the worse the behavior). This gap is important because non-cognitive skills are directly related to what the labor market calls "soft-skills." These skills involve ease of interaction with colleagues and customers, enthusiasm and a positive work attitude—all skills essential in a service driven economy. Thus, if such disparities in social ability exist at such a young age, they can have very negative effects in the future, unless some sort of intervention occurs. In fact, it has been documented that black men are at a particular disadvantage during job interviews, because their body language and communication skills often do not meet employer expectations regarding politeness, indications of motivation, or enthusiasm. . . .

Immigration and Language Disparity

Language disparity plays an important role in wage determination, and according to "Labor Market Costs of Language Disparity: An Interpretation of Hispanic Earnings Differences" explains up to one-third of the relative wage difference between Whites and Hispanics in America. The wage disparity that is usually attributed to ethnicity, nativity, and time in the United States, can in fact be explained by differences associated with English language skills. In the data sample, all the Hispanics were divided into four groups of English proficiency: fluent, very well, well, not well. The findings showed that Hispanic men in the fluent group have earnings insignificantly different from whites who have the same school and potential work experience, as well as residency in the same geographic area. Moving a member of the "very well" group up to full English fluency would raise his wages by 10%, a "well" member to full fluency by 17%, and a "not well" member to fluency by 26%.

Similar results were found in "Why Do Minority Men Earn Less?" Here, the authors found that the status of immigration and whether English is spoken at home both affect earnings. Generally for non-immigrants, if a language other than English is spoken at home, the people earn less than those who speak only English at home. When comparing all immigrants, those who do not speak English at home earn substantially less than those who do. Moreover, when all people who do not speak English at home are compared, the immigrants earn substantially less than non-immigrants. Thus, it can be concluded that one's immigration status as well as what language one speaks at home both affect earnings. When non-immigrants of different racial/ethnic groups who speak English at home are compared, Hispanics and Asians earn just slightly less than whites. However, when all non-immigrants who do not speak English at home are compared, all groups including whites, blacks, Hispanics, and Asians earn about the same with blacks earning slightly more than whites, Hispanics earning slightly less, and Asians earning more. From the data above, it appears that immigrants who do not speak English at home are the lowest earning group in America. Unfortunately, 37% of all Hispanics, and 70% of all Asians in the U.S fall into this category.

Economic Changes

According to the U.S. Department of Labor, there are other things that could affect the wage disparity, and in fact made earnings more unequal during the 1980's and 1990's—these are technological change, trade liberalization, increased immigration, value of the minimum wage, and declining unionization. The economy has transitioned from being driven by manufacturing to information. Thus, as technology continues to advance, the demand for skilled workers who are able to operate the advanced technology and contribute to its development continues to grow. Moreover, technological advancements are causing the replacement of lesser-skilled jobs with automated devices, and thus demand for lesser-skilled workers is dropping. This situation is aggravated by the increase in immigration that has been occurring since 1965. Particularly, less-skilled workers with lower education levels have and continue to immigrate to the U.S., which increases the competition for unskilled jobs and drives wages down for unskilled workers. Expanded trade also drives down the wages of low-skilled workers because it displaces the goods they produce. A decline in unionization in the 1980's has also contributed to increased wage inequality, because fewer workers are benefiting from collective bargaining. Finally, the minimum wage fell in real terms during both the 1970's and 1980's reaching a level in 1990 significantly below its 1960 level.

Understanding Wage Disparity

What does all of this information mean? It is important to have a clear understanding of whether the wage disparity is a result of discrimination in rewarding blacks and Hispanics, or is a result of the disparity in education, skills, hours of work, types of work, and types of job, that exist among different racial and ethnic groups. The distinction is important because the two different explanations have different policy implications. "If persons of identical skill are treated differently on the basis of race or ethnicity, a more vigorous enforcement of civil rights and affirmative action in the market place would appear to be warranted. If the gaps are due to unmeasured abilities and skills that people bring to the labor market, then a redirection of policy towards fostering skills should be emphasized."

The Racial Wage Gap Is Due to Educational Disparities and Occupational Choices

Public Policy Institute of California

The Public Policy Institute of California (PPIC) is a private nonprofit organization dedicated to informing and improving public policy in California through nonpartisan research.

Editor's note: The following viewpoint is taken from a brief summarizing the research report of Deborah Reed and Jennifer Cheng titled "Racial and Ethnic Wage Gaps in the California Labor Market," which was done for the PPIC.

For more than four decades, public policy in the United States has aimed at improving and equalizing opportunity across racial groups through civil rights legislation and affirmative action. When set against this policy backdrop, California's large and persistent wage gaps across racial and ethnic groups remain a concern. In addition to reflecting unequal outcomes in the labor market, these gaps contribute to disparities in other measures of well-being, such as poverty rates, educational attainment, and health status.

In *Racial and Ethnic Wage Gaps in the California Labor Market*, Deborah Reed and Jennifer Cheng investigate these disparities. They find that wage gaps between Latinos, whites, and Asians in the state are largely determined by educational and occupational differences, although these factors account for a smaller portion of the wage gap between African American and white Californians. The authors note that wage gaps stem from factors and worker characteristics not included in the study, and that the findings should therefore not be interpreted as measures of labor market discrimination.

Public Policy Institute of California, "Wage Gaps Between Racial and Ethnic Groups Are Not Diminishing," *Research Brief*, May 2003. www.ppic.org. Reproduced by permission.

Wage Gaps in 2000

Among U.S.-born California full-time workers, the median hourly wage in 2000 for white men was $20.83 and $16.96 for Hispanic men. These medians convert to a relative wage of 81 cents earned by Hispanic men for every dollar earned by white men. For African American men, the median was $15.41, leading to a relative wage of 74 cents on the dollar compared to the wage of white men. Asian men earned a median of $21.82 with a relative wage of $1.04 for every dollar earned by white men.

Compared to white workers, U.S.-born Hispanic workers have lower educational attainment and work in lower-paying occupations.

Among U.S.-born California women who worked full-time, the median wage in 2000 was $17.03 for whites and $13.40 for Hispanics. These medians translate to a relative wage of 79 cents on the dollar for Hispanic women. African American women earned $14.57, which translated to a relative wage of 86 cents on the dollar compared to the wage of white women. The median hourly wage for Asian women was $19.54, or $1.15 for every dollar earned by white women.

Trends in Wage Gaps

For U.S.-born Hispanics, there is no evidence of a substantial change in the wage gap with whites between 1979 and 2000. Hispanic men earned between 81 and 83 cents per dollar earned by white men in each of the three years studied. Hispanic women earned between 79 and 85 cents per dollar earned by white women in each of the years.

For African Americans, there was no substantial change between 1979 and 1989, but relative wages fell between 1989 and 2000. For men, the relative wage at the median was 81 cents per dollar in 1989 and 74 cents in 2000. For women, the wage relative to whites fell from 96 cents per dollar to 86 cents per dollar. In the rest of the nation, the relative wage for African American men did not change substantially between 1989 and 2000 (from 76 to 74 cents per dollar), but for African American women the relative wage fell from 93 to 85 cents per dollar. For U.S.-born Asians, there is also no evidence of substantial changes over recent decades.

What Determines Wage Gaps?

Compared to white workers, U.S.-born Hispanic workers have lower educational attainment and work in lower-paying occupations. Using statistical simulations, the authors conclude that if Hispanic workers had the same education levels as white workers, their relative wages would be substantially higher than they are now: 93 cents per dollar for both men and women. If Hispanics also worked in the same occupations as whites, their wages would be comparable to those of white workers.

On average, African American workers also have less education than white workers and are more likely to work in lower-paying occupations. However, if African American workers had the same education levels as white workers, their relative wages would improve by only a few cents per dollar. If they also worked in the same occupations as whites, their relative wages would improve more substantially, to 84 cents per dollar for men and 95 cents per dollar for women.

U.S.-born Asian workers tend to have higher levels of education than white workers and are more likely to work in higher-paying occupations. If Asian men's education levels matched those of whites, they would not have a wage advantage. For Asian women, matching their education to that of white women would reduce their wage advantage from $1.15 per dollar to $1.09 per dollar and matching the occupations of white women would make little difference to their relative wage.

Prospects and Policy Considerations

The report notes that substantial wage gaps are likely to persist. Wage gaps have not closed in California since the late 1970s, and the growing disparity between the wages of educated and skilled workers and those of workers with low levels of education does not appear to be reversing. Nevertheless, educational attainment for Hispanic and African American workers improved over the 1990s, both in an absolute sense and relative to white workers. The share of Hispanic and African American workers in high-paying occupations also increased. If wage gaps are to decline, the most likely route is through continued improvement in the educational and occupational status of Hispanics and African Americans.

The authors also note that their findings point to general policy directions for reducing racial and ethnic wage gaps. Education and training are important determinants of labor market wages, and their value has increased over the last two decades. Improvements in the quality of K–12 public schools, particularly in underperforming school districts, will likely lead to larger shares of Hispanics and African Americans going to college and eventually to higher wages. California also offers opportunities for students to attend public colleges and universities at relatively low costs, which is particularly important for Hispanic and African American students, whose families tend to have fewer resources than white and Asian families.

The state's efforts to provide worker training through school-to-work programs, welfare-to-work programs, and workforce development are mainly focused on low-educated workers and may therefore be particularly beneficial to Hispanic and African American workers. Recent efforts to encourage early childhood development can improve school readiness, particularly for young Hispanic children, who tend to have low rates of preschool attendance.

In conclusion, the authors maintain that improved opportunities for workers, families, and communities with low resources will reduce racial and ethnic wage gaps in the long run. They also note that the state has much at stake in ensuring that all residents can pursue educational opportunities, enhance their job skills, find good jobs, and support their families.

Chapter 4

Is Education Key to Reducing Wage Gaps?

Chapter Preface

In an effort to reduce cost, Ford Motor Company offered over seventy-five thousand hourly-paid workers buyout packages in 2006. Two of the buyout packages included educational assistance for the displaced workers. Despite this offer, the majority of the displaced workers will either retire or find new jobs.

The Trade Adjustment Assistance Act (TAA) is a federal program created in 1974, long before anyone imagined that U.S. companies such as Ford would face such difficult times. The act was designed to help displaced manufacturing workers who have lost their jobs because of increased imports return to the workforce with new or improved skills. Through the act, displaced workers receive assistance with paying health-care insurance premiums, extended unemployment benefits, tuition, books, and school supplies as they retrain for their next job. Today, displaced Ford workers are utilizing the TAA benefits in combination with their Ford buyout packages to obtain additional funding as they further their educations. In the past, the TAA has helped people like Antonio Ortiz, a displaced Technicolor DVD production plant employee, further his education after losing his position. Today, Ortiz works in the information technology (IT) industry earning more money than he did in his former position, and he has opportunities for career advancement. As Ortiz did, displaced Ford employees are majoring in high demand occupations that pay well.

However, many displaced Ford workers do not see education as their key to future financial security. Sheator Robinson had been employed at the St. Paul, Minnesota, Ford Ranger plant for nineteen years when she learned of the plant's closing in 2007. Although fifty-year-old Robinson earned a BA in business management in 2005 and felt confident that she could find a good job in Minnesota, she opted to transfer her job to a Ford plant in Kansas. Robinson stated, "I didn't want to have to start all over and have to work fifteen to twenty years to get a decent pension." Making the move to Kansas allowed Robinson to stay on track with her retirement plan from Ford that includes a full pension. According to a report from the Government Accountability Office, regardless of whether displaced workers further their education, they will earn approximately 2 percent less than what they earned at their previous jobs. A large majority of the displaced autoworkers believe that it is unlikely that their salaries can be maintained through education. The future looks even bleaker for those who began working in plants decades ago without a high-school diploma. They often need six to eighteen months of schooling just to earn a high school equivalency diploma, or GED.

Globalization has caused countless American workers to lose their jobs due to no fault of their own. However, there is still opportunity for those workers here in America. A 2005 CBS News report, "Blue Collar Jobs Ripe for the Picking," stated that the Labor Department predicts 2.5 million new skilled trade workers will be needed over the next eight years. As displaced Ford workers retrain for their next jobs, many question if education is key to reducing the wage gaps experienced by displaced workers. The viewpoints in the following chapter debate the effect education has on wage gaps.

College-Educated Blacks Are Narrowing the Wage Gap

The Journal of Blacks in Higher Education

The Journal of Blacks in Higher Education *is an issue-oriented publication that examines the progress of African Americans in the nation's colleges and universities.*

New statistics from the Census Bureau confirm the powerful economic advantage that accrues to African Americans who hold a four-year college degree. Current figures for the year 2004 show that blacks with a college diploma now have a median income that is 95 percent of the median income of similarly educated whites. Blacks with a doctorate actually have higher incomes than similarly educated whites. These are extraordinary achievements that have been consistently overlooked by most commentators.

New figures released in late March [2005] by the U.S. Census Bureau unequivocally show that possession of a four-year college degree not only greatly increases the incomes of African Americans but goes almost all the way to close the economic gap between blacks and whites.

[The] statistics show how improved educational attainment advances the incomes of highly educated blacks as compared to those with lower levels of schooling. The first point to note is that blacks with a four-year college degree now earn on average twice the income of blacks who have no better than a high school diploma.

But the new government figures show that even greater value from a *four-year* college degree occurs when we compare incomes of blacks with varying levels of educational achievement. African Americans with a two-year associate's degree

The Journal of Blacks in Higher Education, "Holding a Four-Year College Degree Brings Blacks Close to Economic Parity with Whites," vol. 47, 2005. www.jbhe.com. Reproduced by permission.

improve their income by only 41 percent over blacks with just a high school diploma. But blacks with a four-year college degree outperform blacks with a high school diploma by 99.5 percent. In 2003 blacks with only a high school diploma had a median income of $18,396. The median income of blacks with a bachelor's degree was $36,694.

College Degree Defeats Discrimination

But the important issue is the impact of a college education on the black-white income gap. Here the story is complicated. The *overall median black family income* in the United States is 63 percent of the median white family income. This very large gap in the income ratio has remained virtually unchanged for more than 30 years. Through both good economic times and recessions, there has been little fluctuation in the overall racial income gap. But, one asks, what is the effect of the increase in the number of blacks going to college on the overall black-white income gap? Doesn't this make a difference? The simple answer is, no. It turns out that the much greater earnings produced by more blacks who have completed college make little difference to the *median* income figure (the person in the middle) because only 17.6 percent of all black adults over the age of 25 have completed a four-year college education.

There is a strong demand in the business sector for highly educated African Americans [that] tends to narrow the income gap between the races for those who hold a college diploma.

But now look what happens when we put aside the overall black-white income gap and confine our view only to college-educated blacks and whites. In 2003 blacks with a bachelor's degree had a median income of $36,694. This is 95 percent of the median income of whites with a bachelor's degree, which stood at $38,667.

Corporate America is strongly committed to diversifying its work force and particularly its management ranks. Thus, there is a strong demand in the business sector for highly educated African Americans. This demand tends to narrow the income gap between the races for those who hold a college diploma.

Unfortunately, the encouraging news we report, on the narrowing of the income gap between college-educated blacks and whites, is tempered when we break down the figures by gender and work experience. Separating the statistics by gender, one finds that the superior performance of black women is responsible for most of the good news. In 2003 black males with a bachelor's degree had a median income of $41,916, which was only 82 percent of the $51,138 median income of similarly educated white males. Thus, a very large racial income gap persists for black men who nevertheless have beaten the odds and earned a college degree.

On the other hand, black women with a bachelor's degree had a median income of $33,142, which was 110 percent of the $30,082 median income figure for white women who held a college degree. It is clear then that the strong income performance of black college graduates is largely due to the earnings performance of black women while higher education has failed to produce similar income gains for black men in comparison to white men.

This is not to discount the value of a college degree for black men. African-American men with a bachelor's degree or higher still earn on average nearly double the income of black men with a high school diploma.

Gap Among Educated, Full-Time Workers

The statistics showing the strong earnings performance of black women with a college degree compared to white women with a similar educational background are somewhat misleading. The strong performance of black women is largely explained by the fact that black women college graduates are far more likely to hold full-time jobs than white women college graduates. In 2003 only 48 percent of white women college graduates who had some income held full-time, year-round jobs. Nearly 68 percent of black women college graduates worked full-time. Under these circumstances, it is not surprising that the median income figure for black women college graduates is higher than for white women with a college degree. If we adjust the figures and compare the incomes of white women college graduates who worked full-time with those of similar black women, the traditional racial burden persists. We find from the figures that black women have a median income that is 93 percent that of white women.

Gap for Graduate Degree Holders

The Census Bureau also computes median income figures for blacks and whites with master's and professional degrees. In 2003 blacks with a master's degree had a median income of $44,134. This was 88.3 percent of the median income of whites with a master's degree.

Blacks with a doctorate had a median income of $72,743. This was 111 percent of the median income of whites with doctoral degrees.

Once again, in percentage terms black women fared much better against their white counterparts than did black men. Black and white women with a master's degree had almost identical median incomes, with blacks holding a slight edge. Black men with a master's degree had a median income that was only 82 percent of the median income of white males with a master's degree.

Expectedly, the black-white income gap actually increases for holders of professional degrees. In 2003 blacks with a professional degree had a median income of $61,627. This was only 80 percent of the median income of whites with a professional degree.

It is clear that the economic opportunities for whites with a professional degree continue to be far superior than they are for blacks with a professional degree. White professionals—lawyers, dentists, accountants, and engineers, to name a few—are far more likely to serve economically well-off and better established white clients and therefore are in a position to charge higher fees and earn greater incomes. On the other hand, many whites are still reluctant to seek out the services of black professionals. Therefore, many blacks with professional degrees perform services for an exclusively black clientele and in all likelihood are not able to charge fees comparable to those of white professionals. These factors may explain to some degree the large and often persisting income gap between white and black professionals.

There is also a substantial income gap between blacks and whites who hold doctoral degrees. But this time the racial gap is in favor of blacks. In 2003 blacks with a doctorate had a median income of $72,743. This was 111 percent of the median income of whites with doctoral degrees, which stands at $65,278. The high demand for black academics at American colleges and universities produces a good job market with high wages for blacks with doctoral degrees.

A final consideration: Favorable statistics on the black-white income gap for college graduates always must be viewed in light of the fact that black college graduates make up only a small portion of the entire black population of the United States. According to the latest count, there are 36.4 million people in the United States whom the Census Bureau classifies as black. Of these, 3,854,000, or less than 11 percent, hold a four-year college degree. Therefore, one must always keep in mind that the encouraging economic figures we report here apply to only one in every nine African Americans.

Hispanics Earning Science and Engineering Degrees Can Narrow the Wage Gap

Margaret Loftus

Margaret Loftus is a writer based in Charleston, South Carolina. A former U.S. News & World Report *staffer, she writes regularly on travel as a contributing editor at* National Geographic Traveler.

A s a young boy growing up in Cuba, Oscar Garcia loved to tinker with radios, but it wasn't until he got a toy motor kit for Christmas that he was bitten by the engineering bug. With the instructions for assembling the motor in English, the 12-year-old Garcia enlisted the help of an electrical engineering student who lived down the street from his family. "He and I put it together," remembers Garcia, "but it didn't work, so I was very chagrined." He wouldn't be deterred, however, and worked on it himself until it purred. "That was the turning point. I decided I was a natural for electrical engineering." Garcia went on to an illustrious career that has included designing computers for IBM, a stint at the National Science Foundation and his current post as dean of the College of Engineering at the University of North Texas.

An Exception to the Rule

But as a Hispanic-American, Garcia is an exception to the rule. While they are the largest minority group in the United States at 14.5 percent of the population, only 4 percent of engineers in the workforce in this country are Hispanic. Just 7 percent of the bachelor's degrees in engineering, 5 percent of master's degrees and even fewer doctoral degrees are awarded to Hispanics. Meanwhile, the Hispanic birthrate and immigration continue to outpace those of African-Americans and non-Hispanic whites: The U.S. Latino population is expected to grow 45 percent by 2015, compared with 1 percent for whites. With the chasm threatening to grow even wider in just a few short years, many engineering educators say that attracting more Hispanics to engineering and engineering education is no longer a choice. . . .

Hispanic-American Wages

Another factor is pure economics. In previous waves of immigration, there were more opportunities for unskilled workers. Hispanics account for more than 40 percent of all high school dropouts in the United States. In the past, these kids may have gone on to make a fair wage in the manufacturing sector. "You didn't have to go to school to earn a decent wage," [New Mexico State University College of Engineering dean Steven] Castillo says.

The best predictor of a student's success in college is related to the rigor of math courses they took in high school.

Today is a whole other story: The United States will lose 7 million jobs in manufacturing in the next 10 years, with the same number of jobs being added in technology. As a result, immigrants and first-generation Americans can no longer afford not to have a college degree. Growing up in a small rural town south of Albuquerque, Castillo says he had a lot of smart Hispanic friends who didn't go to college because their family valued work over education or they just plain couldn't afford it. And while the idea of forgoing a college degree to work may seem short-sighted to some, others see it as doing the right thing. "The idea of helping your family is very prevalent [in Hispanic cultures]," Garcia explains—making it tough to convince high school kids and their parents that college is important and doubly tough to push graduate school. . . .

Making Math Add Up

Of course, a curriculum rich in STEM (science, technology, engineering and math) subjects is one thing; getting kids to enroll in those courses is quite another. "Many high school students don't recognize the value in math and intentionally go in the direction that minimizes the need for it. This goes across the board for all ethnicities, but you see it more in economically depressed areas," argues Hector Carrasco, engineering dean at Colorado State University–Pueblo, where Hispanics make up more than one-fourth of the engineering school. Not only is a solid math background essential to majoring in engineering, he says, "The best predictor of a student's success in college is related to the rigor of math courses they took in high school." That's why Carrasco's department assigns student mentors to schools in Pueblo where there's a high percentage of kids from lower income families. The mentors tutor students as young as sixth graders in math and talk up college and financial aid opportunities.

Likewise, Wichita State has a co-advising program with middle and high school guidance counselors to help students choose coursework wisely, particularly math, so they won't be at a disadvantage when it comes to higher education. [Zulma] Toro-Ramos, for one, knows how important this is: As an eighth grader in Puerto Rico she enrolled in a probability and statistics course as part of a government experiment. The class sparked her interest in math, which led to her career as an engineer. As part of her plan to boost the number of Hispanics majoring in engineering at WSU, she's also proposed a partnership with the Wichita school district to educate Hispanic students and their parents about the opportunities in higher education and stem fields. "For Hispanics, it's very difficult to leave their communities and go somewhere else. If the institution is not in their backyard, it will be tough, so we have to reach out to them."

To this end, several universities host summer camps to expose young Hispanics and other minorities to stem subjects. New Mexico State University's College of Engineering, for instance, brings 180 middle and high school students to campus each summer for intense math and science workshops. "We target demographics that we really want to push engineering on," says Castillo, who became interested in engineering himself at a summer camp at rival University of New Mexico. "It's been an extremely successful program for us."

On top of formal programs, [University of California]–Davis's [Enrique] Lavernia stresses the power of role models. He meets with K–12 students as much as possible. "Typically a dean doesn't do this, but being Hispanic gives me access to them that's not typical." NSF [National Science Foundation] has helped by funding the recruitment of community college students, among whom his heritage resonates. "Many transfer students from community colleges are minorities. They see UC-Davis as too intimidating. I try to dispel that perception." He also welcomes visits from younger students, describing a recent encounter with 70 fifth and sixth graders from a nearby largely Hispanic school district. "That's when you really need to capture them, tell them they can do it, particularly female Hispanic students who have very few role models," Lavernia says. . . .

Academia: A Hard Sell

Another challenge not unique to Hispanics but possibly more prevalent is attracting them to graduate school and into academia. When Lavernia told his father that he wanted to become a professor, his father—an engineer himself—jokingly chided him for "not wanting to work for a living." Castillo explains that parents often present the largest obstacle when it comes to encouraging promising undergrads to pursue academia as a career. "Parents say, 'Why are you doing this? Go out and make money.'" Indeed, the salaries dangled in front of freshly minted engineers are hard to pass up, especially for someone who may have come from an underprivileged background or has racked up unwieldy student loans.

Some programs are working to counter this, such as the NSF-funded Bridge to the Doctorate program that specifically targets minority students, offering fellowships and assisting them in applying to Ph.D. programs around the country. And at Michigan State University's College of Engineering, an initiative with support from the Alfred P. Sloan Foundation is focused on recruiting and mentoring Hispanic engineering grad students. As a result, the past seven years have seen an increase of 36 percent in the enrollment of African-American and Hispanic doctoral students and a retention rate of 90 percent.

While these incremental successes are promising, the deans agree that much work remains. [Louis] Martin-Vega says that stressing the breadth of engineering is crucial to attracting more Hispanics to the field. Growing up in Puerto Rico where several engineers were in prominent government positions, Martin-Vega credits these role models with his own interest in engineering. "The message I received was that an engineering degree would provide you with a career in many professional endeavors and not just highly technical careers." Indeed, research has shown that service-oriented work is more attractive to under-represented minorities. "Usually Hispanics see engineering as a very dry profession. One that doesn't really deal with people," explains Toro-Ramos, which is why she has developed a bioengineering program at WSU. "If they know that they will have the opportunities to work with communities, that will attract them more."

Lavernia believes there's room for optimism. "This is a portion of the population that can use engineering as an incredible stepping stone, but they need help. It behooves us to be aggressive."

Women Earn More than Men Just Out of College

Sam Roberts

Sam Roberts is a New York Times *reporter and host of NY-1's cable talk show* New York Close-Up. *He is the author of* Who We Are: A Portrait of America Based on the Latest U.S. Census.

Young women in New York and several of the nation's other largest cities who work full time have forged ahead of men in wages, according to an analysis of recent census data.

The shift has occurred in New York since 2000 and even earlier in Los Angeles, Dallas and a few other cities.

Economists consider it striking because the wage gap between men and women nationally has narrowed more slowly and has even widened in recent years among one part of that group: college-educated women in their 20s. But in New York, young college-educated women's wages as a percentage of men's rose slightly between 2000 and 2005.

The analysis was prepared by Andrew Beveridge, a demographer at Queens College, who first reported his findings in *Gotham Gazette*, published online by the Citizens Union Foundation. It shows that all women from 21 to 30 living in New York City and working full time made 117 percent of men's wages, and even more in Dallas, 120 percent.

Nationwide, that group of women made much less: 89 percent of the average full-time pay for men.

Education and the Wage Gap

Just why young women at all educational levels in New York and other big cities have fared better than their peers elsewhere is a matter of some debate. But a major reason, experts

Sam Roberts, "Shift Emerges in Wage Gap Between the Sexes," *International Herald Tribune*, August 3, 2007. Reproduced with permission.

say, is that women have been graduating from college in larger numbers than men, and that many of those women seem to be gravitating toward major urban areas.

In 2005, 53 percent of women in their 20s working in New York were college graduates, compared with only 38 percent of men of that age.

And many of those women are not marrying right after college, leaving them freer to focus on building careers, experts said.

"Citified college women are more likely to be nonmarried and childless, compared with their suburban sisters, so they can and do devote themselves to their careers," said Andrew Hacker, a Queens College sociologist and the author of *Mismatch: The Growing Gulf Between Men and Women*.

Kelly Kraft, 25, is one of those women. A native of Indiana, she came to New York after graduating from the University of Dayton, got a job in publishing and now works for an advertising agency. "I just felt New York had a lot more exciting opportunities in different industries than Indianapolis," she said.

As women enrolled in college and graduate school continue to outnumber men, gender wage gaps among older workers may narrow, too.

"In women's studies courses you always heard that men were making more money, and it was a disadvantage being a woman," Kraft said. "It's great that it's starting to turn around."

New York may also be more attractive to college-educated women, some experts said, because many jobs in the city pay higher salaries than similar ones elsewhere in the country. "New York is an achievement-based city, and achievement here is based on how well you use your brain, not what you do with your back," said Mitchell Moss, a professor of urban policy and planning at the Robert F. Wagner Graduate School of Public Service at New York University.

In 1970, all New York women in their 20s made $7,000 less than men, on average, adjusted for inflation. By 2000, they were about even. In 2005, according to an analysis of the latest census results, they were making about $5,000 more: a median wage of $35,653, or 117 percent of the $30,560 reported by men in that age group.

Women in their 20s also make more than men in Chicago, Boston, Minneapolis and a few other big cities. But only in Dallas do young women's wages surpass men's by a larger amount than in New York. In Dallas, women make 120 percent of what men do, although their median wage there, $25,467, was much lower than that of women in New York.

Nationally, women in their 20s made a median income of $25,467, compared with $28,523 for men.

Diana Rhoten, a program director at the Social Science Research Council in New York, said well-educated women were migrating to urban centers where there are diverse professional opportunities and less gender discrimination than in smaller cities and suburbs. There may also be nonworkplace factors at play, she said.

Career Strategy

"Previously, female migration patterns were determined primarily by their husband's educational levels or employment needs, even if both were college-educated," she said. "Today, highly qualified women are moving for their own professional opportunities and personal interests. It's no longer an era of power couple migration to, but one of power couple formation in, places like New York."

Beveridge based his findings of young women's earning power on data from the census bureau's 2005 American Community Survey used to analyze people working at least 35 hours a week, 40 or more weeks a year.

It is not clear whether this is the front edge of a trend in which women will gradually move ahead of men in all age groups. Typically, women have fallen further behind men in earnings as they get older.

That is because some women stop working altogether, work only part time or encounter a glass ceiling in promotions and raises.

But as women enrolled in college and graduate school continue to outnumber men, gender wage gaps among older workers may narrow, too, experts said. Even among New Yorkers in their 30s, women now make as much as men.

Melissa Manfro, a 24-year-old lawyer who was raised in upstate New York, offered her own theory on why younger female lawyers are outearning their male peers: a desire to begin their careers earlier to prepare for starting families.

"It seems that women tend to take less time off between college and law school, and therefore become more senior, and, hence, make more money, at a younger age," she said. "I would, of course, like to think that means that women know what they want sooner than men. But it probably has more to do with the unfortunate fact that women need to keep in mind biological time constraints and feel a great deal of pressure to build an entire career before refocusing on marriage and children."

Though Beveridge's analysis showed women making strides, it also showed that men were in some ways moving backward. Among all men—including those with college degrees—real wages, adjusted for inflation, have declined since 1970. And among full-time workers with advanced degrees, wages for men increased only marginally even as they soared for women. Nationally, men's wages in general declined while women's remained the same.

Several experts also said that rising income for women might affect marriage rates if women expect their mates to have at least equivalent salaries and education.

"When New York college women say there are few eligible men around, they're right if they mean they'll only settle for someone with an education akin to their own," Hacker said.

Women Earn Less than Their Male Counterparts Just a Year Out of College

Amy Joyce

Amy Joyce writes a Washington Post *column, "Life at Work on Sundays," and hosts an online weekly chat on interpersonal issues in the workplace.*

For years, women have outnumbered men on college campuses. Overall, they get better grades than men. And yet, just months after they toss their mortarboards into the air at college graduation, men start to pull ahead of women in pay.

Though the pay gap between men and women is well documented, it is startling to discover that it begins so soon. According to a new study by the American Association of University Women [AAUW], women already earn 20 percent less than men at the same level and in the same field one year after college graduation. Right at the beginning, before taking time off for childbirth or child-rearing, women find themselves behind.

Of course, it only gets worse. Today, women earn about 77 cents for every dollar a man earns, according to Census data, a figure that has remained steady for about a decade. The gap is deeply entrenched. The AAUW started studying the disparity in 1913, documenting different pay for men and women among federal government workers.

Ten years after graduation, women fall further behind, earning 69 percent of what men earn.

The latest study is unusual because it devotes attention to the first year out of school. "We are looking at a younger group of people who have many similarities," said Catherine Hill, director of research for the AAUW. "When they are just coming out of college, we expect to see fewer differences."

The gap, starting early, only widens as time goes on, according to the AAUW report "Behind the Pay Gap." Ten years after graduation, women fall further behind, earning 69 percent of what men earn. A 12 percent gap appeared even when the AAUW Educational Foundation, which did the research, controlled for hours, occupation, parenthood and other factors known to directly affect earnings.

The remainder of the gap is unexplained by any other control factors. That may mean, Hill said, that discrimination is the root cause. . . .

Taking Action

While discrimination accounts for some of the discrepancy, said Linda Babcock, James M. Walton professor of economics at Carnegie Mellon University, women also suffer because they have not been taught to ask for more. Babcock, co-author of *Women Don't Ask: Negotiation and the Gender Divide*, argues that women don't negotiate enough, or many times, at all. She is not blaming women for creating their own wage gap, she said, but rather, society, for raising "little girls to accept the status quo."

Babcock encountered such an example while watching one of her daughter's favorite television shows, "Dragon Tales," an animated PBS series where a human brother and sister visit friends in Dragon Land. In one episode, the sister wants to make friends with a group of dragon scouts. Instead of just asking, Babcock said, the girl used indirect ways to fit in. She eventually succeeded by urging the scouts to join in teamwork.

For Babcock, the show reflected reality: Women are brought up to avoid asking for anything directly.

And so what can women do?

For one, realize that it's not your fault, Babcock said. "It's liberating that it's not some inherent piece of my personality that I do this. Those are the voices that have been in my head over the years."

In a widely cited study from 1979, first-, fourth-, seventh- and 10th-graders were given a set task, then asked to pay themselves based on how well they thought they did. There was no difference between the sexes in the evaluations, but researchers found that in every grade, girls paid themselves 30 percent to 78 percent less than boys did.

Negotiation Skills

Babcock said women should use a "cooperative negotiation style" to get what they want.

For example, don't go to a manager and say, "I have another job offer and unless you match it, I'll leave." That approach would be seen as threatening from a woman, even if it could be accepted from a man, Babcock said. So instead, reframe it: "I have this other offer, but I'd like to find a way to stay here. Can you match it so I can stay?"

Babcock also suggests practice. It may take a while for a woman to get over what she has been taught. So before negotiating, try some role-playing, she said. If you don't, you may ask for a raise and concede too fast or not negotiate at all. To prepare, sit with a colleague who knows the boss. Then go through different scenarios and ways to negotiate until you become comfortable with the process, she said. "We get most anxious when we don't know what to expect."

And once women know a little about what to expect, they may consider asking for what they want, as their male counterparts typically do.

Babcock conducted a study in 2002 that looked at starting salaries of students graduating from Carnegie Mellon University with master's degrees. The starting salaries of men were 7.6 percent higher, or almost $4,000 more, on average, than those of the women. It turned out, however, that only 7 percent of the female students had negotiated, but 57 percent of the men had asked for more money. The students who negotiated increased their starting salaries by 7.4 percent on average, or $4,053. That's almost exactly the difference between men's and women's average starting pay.

A lack of negotiating skills could be a part of the reason for the wage gap, said Hill of the AAUW report. Or it could go back to the person doing the listening. "Two workers who use the same kind of language could be perceived differently." In other words, a man and a woman might ask for the same thing in the same way, but get a different result.

In many cases, even women who finally ask for a raise may not get it because decision-makers aren't used to accepting negotiating behavior from women, Babcock said.

"Our society has a real double standard about what's acceptable for women to do and men to do," she said. "We're perfectly fine accepting negotiating behavior from men, but we react negatively when a woman does that. She knows she'll get a negative response or that we'll judge her, so she holds back."

At least two recent polls show that is likely happening. In another of Babcock's studies, she found 20 percent of women polled said they never negotiate at all. And in a recent study conducted by *PINK* magazine, a career publication for women, nearly half of 2,400 women surveyed didn't ask for a raise or promotion in the previous 12 months.

However, of those who did ask, 72 percent received one.

Knowing that, perhaps a few more women can gain some ground. And they just might set off enough change that today's young girls won't need to worry about a gap at all.

Blacks with Education Equal to Whites' Still Experience a Wage Gap

Curtis Lawrence

Curtis Lawrence is a journalism professor at Columbia College in Chicago.

Even advanced academic degrees don't shrink the salary gap between the nation's black and white males, new census figures show.

Whether they have high school diplomas or master's degrees, black men still earn roughly 25 percent less than whites at the same education level, according to 2002 census figures.

The median income for a black man with a high school diploma was $27,224 in 2002. A white man with the same education made $35,738, about 24 percent more. The median income for black men with a master's degree was $50,763, compared with $69,655 for whites—a 27 percent difference.

Hiring and Promotions

One explanation for the gap is discrimination in the workplace. Others say the gap comes from the overall lower quality of education for blacks, regional disparities in pay or that blacks on average choose jobs that typically pay less, such as teaching or social work.

Emmett Vaughn calls the discrepancy the "opportunity gap," meaning black men are simply not given the same chances when it comes to hiring and promotions.

"As I look at my graduating class, I know some white counterparts who are already officers of companies, and I can say seriously that the brothers aren't there," said Vaughn, who graduated from Northwestern University's Kellogg School of Management in 2001 with an MBA and is now in charge of minority business development for [supermarket chain] Albertson's, the parent company of Jewel-Osco.

The reasons for the gap are too complex to boil down to racism or discrimination, said Vaughn. But "comfort, risk and race" definitely come into play when hiring and promotions are made, he said.

"I think there's a perception that there's less risk in giving more responsibility to a white person than to a black person."

But others, such as Dave Diersen, a white accountant from Wheaton [just west of Chicago] who is part of a class-action discrimination suit against the U.S. General Accounting Office, feel that there are plenty of opportunities for black men and other minorities.

Black women with a high school degree earned about 12 percent less than white women. Black women with master's degrees earned about 6 percent less than white women.

"I'm arguing that there is not only equality [for blacks and minorities] in the office where I worked, but that there was preferences given to minorities and females because of affirmative action mandates," Diersen said.

Diersen is now treasurer of Adversity.net, a nonprofit group that promotes discussions about the impact of racial preferences. He claims he suffered under policies designed to advance minorities and women and was forced out in 1997 after complaining.

Causes of the Wage Gap

Economics Professor Derek Neal of the University of Chicago and William R. Johnson from the University of Virginia point to the quality of education between blacks and whites, not the number of years of schooling the census figures show.

While some of the gap is due to labor market discrimination, "most of it is attributed to different skills they are bringing to the labor market, even if they have the same years of education," Johnson said.

When Johnson and Neal studied the wage gap between black and white men in the mid-1990s, they reduced it to 7 percent when they took early-schooling test scores into account.

Neal cautioned that the census figures also don't include the many African Americans with little education who are not in the labor market. If those numbers were included, the gap at the lower end of the education scale would be much wider, Neal said.

Others have conducted their own studies of the wage discrepancy.

Professor William Rodgers, who teaches public policy and is a chief economist at the John J. Heldrich Center for Workforce Development at Rutgers University, examined earnings from 1999 to 2002 and found an unexplained wage gap of 17.3 percent between black and white men in executive, administrative and managerial occupations. Similar salary gaps of 16.1 percent and 16.3 percent, respectively, existed in sales occupations and professional specialty occupations such as teaching and accounting.

Contributing to the gap, said Rodgers, is that "labor market discrimination is still a key feature of the black experience."

The gaps in Rodgers' studies are smaller than in the census reports because he made adjustments for regional salary disparities and other factors that may have artificially widened the gap.

Black women have similar wage-gap discrepancies, but the gap is not as wide. Black women with a high school degree earned about 12 percent less than white women. Black women with master's degrees earned about 6 percent less than white women.

Bernard Loyd, who recently left McKinsey & Co.—a high-profile international consulting firm—to staff his own business, said African-American men can't cash in at the rate of whites because they still have trouble getting in the doors of high-profile firms.

"The first set of issues is at the entry point. Many prestigious firms have not been particularly hospitable to minorities and to blacks in particular," said Loyd, 41, who joined McKinsey in 1990—only the fifth black full-time consultant to be hired in the Chicago office.

Loyd, who earned an MBA and a doctorate in engineering from the Massachusetts Institute of Technology, became a partner at McKinsey in 1998. While McKinsey has made efforts to level the playing field, the corporate world as a whole still has work to do, Loyd said.

Even after they get in the door, blacks rarely stay on promotion track at the same pace as their white counterparts, Loyd said. "As a result, we are largely shut off from the positions of influence and compensation that would allow us to earn our share."

College Degrees Widen Economic Inequality

Stuart Tannock

Stuart Tannock is a lecturer in social and cultural studies in the Graduate School of Education at the University of California, Berkeley.

Is it possible that our thinking on the question of college access and economic inequality is back to front? At a time when some young Americans are quite literally dying to go to college—the primary reason now cited by young recruits for enlisting in the U.S. military is their desire to obtain financial assistance for college—we need to take a serious second look at what is being said and done with higher education and young people in this country. Now that alternative historical avenues for social and economic advancement (for example, industry-wide unionization and expanding public sector employment) have been shut down or obstructed, going to college remains the only legitimate, large-scale means for getting ahead. Yet even as demand for college education swells across the nation, the sobering truth is that college, in its current form at least, can help only a few of us resolve our labor market difficulties. According to the U.S. Bureau of Labor Statistics, no more than 30 percent of jobs in the United States currently, and for the foreseeable future, will require a college degree. . . .

The College/Non-College Wage Gap

I look at one piece of the overall problem—the wage gap between the college and non-college educated in America—in order to suggest some of the directions that this larger conversation must explore. . . .

The average wage gap is important for three reasons. First, the gap grew exponentially over the last third of the twentieth century, and, though it has shown some signs of leveling off recently, it remains both sizable and salient. Second, this gap helps us to understand the behavior of many people in contemporary America. Students are firmly oriented to the gap: the number one reason college freshmen give today for pursuing higher education is to get a good job and secure a higher standard of living. Colleges actively promote this gap: they market themselves to prospective applicants by pointing to the doors they open into lucrative employment. K–12 educators are fixated on this gap: the highest purpose of high school— and even elementary and preschool—is to prepare students for college. And politicians are highly aware of this gap: to succeed economically in this country, so they all say, it has become a virtual requirement to obtain a college degree.

To call for increased opportunities for young Americans to go to college ... is wrongheaded and unjust.

The third reason for focusing on the wage gap is that it provides a simple and shorthand way of tracking what colleges are doing in our society and economy. And so it enables us to hold colleges and universities, as well as graduates and professionals, accountable for their role in the production and reproduction of inequality.

College Education Not a Cure-All

The dominant public response to the wage gap has been to call for increased opportunities for young Americans to go to college....

Despite this near-universal consensus, the dominant response to the wage gap is wrongheaded and unjust. It is wrongheaded because only a minority of jobs in the United States require a college degree. It is unjust because it accepts the wage gap as natural, inevitable, and legitimate—rather than treating it as something to be questioned and challenged. Given the actual distribution of jobs in the country, this response tacitly condones relegating the majority of Americans to a lifetime of work in low-wage, poor-quality jobs, and makes K–12 schooling into little more than a vast sorting system for identifying each generation's economic winners and losers. By focusing our attention on the false promise of increased educational attainment as a cure-all for inequality in America, it diverts energies from the underlying sources of injustice.

Universities fail to serve the public good when they increase primarily the wages, wealth, and well-being of their own students, while leaving everyone else further and further behind.

We need to turn our thinking about higher education and inequality completely around. Currently, leftists, liberals, and conservatives all tend to applaud the role that college plays in increasing the earnings of the college educated. But what if we were to view the growing wage gap not as a sign of success in higher education but of failure? What if we were to frame the gap as a public bad, and stigmatize it? Finally, what if we were to see the task of narrowing this gap—in ways that were socially just—as something to which we should all dedicate our energies, whether we are in the academy or without? In this way, we could begin to shift our politics away from the errant task of trying to get everyone into college, toward the more genuinely democratic task of building solidarity and equality among all individuals, irrespective of educational or occupational status. . . .

Higher Education and the Public Good

Since the beginning of this country, public and private institutions of higher education have received extensive public financial support, in the form of direct subsidy and investment, as well as through tax breaks to college students and their families and tax exemptions to colleges and their donors. Unlike with primary and secondary schools, we have never expected colleges (particularly four-year colleges) to serve directly all individuals in the country—including the shift, in the period following the Second World War, from an "elite" to a so-called "mass" or "universal" model of higher education. But we have expected—and we should expect—that, in return for public support, colleges will benefit all of us, even if indirectly, regardless of whether we go to college or not. . . .

Universities serve the public good, all else being equal, not when they contribute to "economic development" in some abstract and general sense, but when they help to increase the wealth and well-being of all individuals together; and more specifically, when they work to ensure that the college-educated do not gain at the expense of the non-college-educated. Universities fail to serve the public good when they increase primarily the wages, wealth, and well-being of their own students, while leaving everyone else further and further behind. If universities are unable—or worse, unwilling—to tackle such issues as the wage gap, then perhaps a compelling public-good argument can be made that the non-college-educated in this country (that is, the majority of the population) would be better off spending their tax dollars on themselves directly, rather than allowing them to be siphoned through an increasingly expensive, elitist, unresponsive, and uncivic system of national higher education.

Narrowing the Gap

We have been taught by human-capital theory to link more education with more pay. We have been disciplined by neoliberal ideology to believe that wage distribution must be left to the market, that there are no alternatives available, and that inequality is inevitable. Elements of truth exist, of course, in both of these views; but the whole truth can be found in neither.

Education is not linked in all cases with increased income . . . nor does it have to be so linked in any single case. The signaling function that formal education plays in assigning pay levels in our credentialist society can be (and frequently has been) challenged; and the content of education can shape different social and economic outcomes. Markets, meanwhile, work the way they do because they have been organized and legislated to work this way; they can always be re-organized and re-legislated. We should remember, after all, that it is almost without exception the college-educated who design and implement our market policy. . . .

Positions of status, power, voice, and meaningful employment are currently just too few in number to be made available to everybody.

More fundamentally, though, universities have an impact on the wage gap—along with many other inequalities in wealth and health indicators that go along with it—primarily through their decisions about which educational agendas and research concerns take priority. It is not just through figuring out how to raise the wages of the non-college-educated (that is, bringing up the bottom) that universities can work toward narrowing the gap, but also through curbing the perceived need, the desire, and perhaps the ability, of their own graduates to earn astronomically high incomes. Indeed, it is precisely the linking of these two, the conditions at the top and bottom, that is essential in any serious effort to achieve greater economic equality. . . .

Over the last couple of decades, college tuition and individual student debt in the United States have skyrocketed. The ramifications of rising costs and debt have been considered primarily in terms of college access—who is and is not able to afford higher education in this country. Increasingly, the poor and working classes are less likely than wealthier classes to attend college and get a degree, not just because of their lack of the skills and knowledge necessary to get into higher education but also because of a sheer lack of financial capacity.

Unequal college access is an issue of great importance. However, we need to consider as well the public good effects of tuition and debt levels not just on who gets into college, but also on what college students do once they leave the university campus, degree in hand. . . .

Beyond Economism and Nationalism

First, it is not just a difference in wealth and wage levels that separates the college- from the non-college-educated. It is also the many intrinsic rewards often associated with those social positions to which a college degree provides access. Status, power, voice, opportunities for meaningful employment and participation: in all these areas a gap exists between the college- and non-college-educated that mirrors the gap in wage levels.

If we cannot think of ways to address these kinds of inequalities, we risk finding ourselves right back where we started. For it would then be unjust to deny individuals the opportunity to go to college, and at the same time, it would be misguided to expect that universal college enrollment could ever successfully resolve these inequalities. Positions of status, power, voice, and meaningful employment are currently just too few in number to be made available to everybody.

Second, we must address the nationalist framework that I have allowed to shape my discussion thus far. Some would argue, contrary to my assertions here, that college education can in fact help everyone in America gain access to high-wage employment. This is the argument of Robert Reich in his 1991 book *The Work of Nations*. Work today, he says, can be divided into three broad categories: "routine production services" and "in-person services," both of which are increasingly likely to be poorly paid; and "symbolic analyst" work (by which Reich means the work of professionals, managers, and the college-educated), which continues to be relatively highly paid. What Reich proposes as a sound development strategy—and what many countries around the world have, in fact, been attempting in recent years—is to pursue a nationalist education and economic agenda that seeks to monopolize as many of the world's high-paying symbolic analyst jobs as possible, while shunting off production and in-person service to citizens from other countries, whether they work domestically or overseas. The United States, and the developed Organization for Economic Cooperation and Development countries generally, already hold a disproportionate share of the world's college jobs; and universities and nations around the globe are competing with one another to secure an ever-larger piece of the higher education pie.

If we are to develop a comprehensive vision of how higher education should serve the public good, we must, of course, reject as shortsighted and unjust such forms of nationalist competition. We must make sure that when we speak of inequality, we are thinking of it at a worldwide level. And we must, hard as this is to conceptualize, include in our vision of the "public" and the "public good" the college- and non-college-educated not just of our own country but across the planet.

There has been, over the past decade, much talk of the need to build international labor solidarity to head off a devastating "race to the bottom." But little has been said about how we should work internationally to avert a potentially equally devastating "race to the top." Without attention to both of these races, "internationalism" and "global labor solidarity" will amount to little more than well-intentioned, but empty political rhetoric.

The Paradox

Without a vision of what higher education should look like in a just world, it will be hard for us to move toward justice.

Even with such a vision, we still face the vexing issue of how to advance. Too often, talk of serving the public good on university campuses these days proceeds as if such work were little more than a happy series of camera-friendly photo-ops designed to demonstrate the bubbling over of university-community synergies. A serious commitment to battle inequality along the lines envisioned here means that we will have an enormous fight on our hands.

There are places, though, to dig in and get started. The college/non-college wage gap provides a useful metric for assessing shifts in the impact that higher education is having on inequality in society. The legitimation crisis in higher education provides an opening for broadening the conversation about what we should really be asking of our colleges and universities. Public funding of higher education provides leverage in support of demands we wish to place on higher education. The U.S. Supreme Court *Bob Jones* decision of 1983—in which Bob Jones University was stripped of its tax-exempt status on the grounds that its racism was in violation of "fundamental national public policy"—provides, if not legal precedent, then at least a conceptual model for pressuring universities to serve the public good.

In an essay on "Equality of Opportunity, and Beyond," John Schaar quotes Matthew Arnold as saying that "equality will never of itself alone give us a perfect civilization. But, with such inequality as ours, a perfect civilization is impossible." This may be the paradox of rethinking the relationship that education now bears to the economy. By working diligently to reduce the impact of education on wealth and wages, we can free educational institutions to foster the kind of teaching and learning that could, in the long run, produce a much more radical re-visioning of our world than is possible right now—socially, culturally, politically, and also economically.

Organizations to Contact

The editors have compiled the following list of organizations concerned with the issues debated in this book. The descriptions are derived from materials provided by the organizations. All have publications or information available for interested readers. The list was compiled on the date of publication of the present volume; the information provided here may change. Readers need to remember that many organizations take several weeks or longer to respond to inquiries.

American Association of University Women
1111 Sixteenth St. NW, Washington, DC   20036
(800) 326-2289 • fax: (202) 872-1425
e-mail: helpline@aauw.org
Web site: www.aauw.org

The American Association of University Women advances equity for women and girls through advocacy, education, and research. Since its founding in 1881, members have examined and taken positions on the fundamental issues of the day—educational, social, economic, and political. "Women at Work," a report by the AAUW Educational Foundation, combines interview and survey data with recent U.S. census statistics to explore how women are faring in today's workforce and what their prospects are for future job success and security.

American Federation of Labor-Congress of Industrial Organizations (AFL-CIO)
815 Sixteenth St. NW, Washington, DC   20006
Web site: www.aflcio.org

The American Federation of Labor and Congress of Industrial Organizations is a voluntary federation of fifty-five national and international labor unions. The mission of the AFL-CIO is to improve the lives of working families—to bring economic justice to the workplace and social justice to our nation. *America@work*, the official publication of the AFL-CIO, is designed to inspire and support frontline union leaders and activists with tips, tools, and news to help build a strong voice for America's working families.

Civilrights.org

1629 K St. NW, 10th Fl., Washington, DC 20006
(202) 466-331
Web site: www.civilrights.org

Civilrights.org serves as the site of record for relevant and up-to-the-minute civil rights news and information. Home to socially concerned, issue-oriented original audio, video, and written programming, Civilrights.org is committed to serving as the online nerve center not only for the struggle against discrimination in all its forms, but also to build the public understanding that it is essential for our nation to continue its journey toward social and economic justice. Civilrights.org features include the *Daily Buzz*, an e-mail news service delivered Monday–Friday; *This Week in Civil Rights*, an overview of each week's civil rights news, information and events; and the *Civil Rights Monitor*, a quarterly publication that reports on civil rights issues pending before the three branches of government.

Community Teamwork, Inc. (CTI)

167 Dutton St., Lowell, MA 01852
(978) 459-0551 • fax: (978) 453-9128
Web site: www.comteam.org

Community Teamwork, Inc. strives to assist low-income people to become self-sufficient, to alleviate the effects of poverty, and to assist low-income people to participate in the decisions that affect their lives. CTI works as an advocate and catalyst for systemic change on issues that affect low-income people, including education, workforce training, housing, economic development, and civic engagement. CTI publishes a quarterly newsletter, *CTI Ink*.

National Association for the Advancement of Colored People (NAACP)

4805 Mt. Hope Dr., Baltimore, MD   21215

(410) 580-5777

Web site: www.naacp.org

The mission of the National Association for the Advancement of Colored People is to ensure the political, educational, social, and economic equality of rights of all persons and to eliminate racial hatred and racial discrimination. The NAACP is an advocacy organization that fights for the advancement of minority groups by bridging the gaps in seven advocacy areas, including education, economic empowerment, health care, criminal justice, civic engagement, international affairs, and poverty issues. The *Crisis Magazine* is the official publication of the NAACP and is dedicated to being an open and honest forum for discussing critical issues confronting people of color, American society, and the world in addition to highlighting the historical and cultural achievements of these diverse peoples.

National Association for Female Executives (NAFE)

(212) 255-8455 ext 22 • fax: (212) 255-8455

e-mail: kate@rosengrouppr.com

Web site: www.nafe.com

The National Association for Female Executives, founded in 1972, is the largest women's professional association and the largest women business owners' organization in the country, providing resources and services through education, networking, and public advocacy to empower its members to achieve career success and financial security. The NAFE conference and special events division produce a 100 Best Companies WorkLife Conference, the Best Companies for Women of Color Conference, and the NAFE National Conference. NAFE is owned by Working Mother Media (WMM), which includes *Working Mother* and *NAFE Magazine*.

National Bureau of Economic Research, Inc. (NBER)
1050 Massachusetts Ave., Cambridge, MA   02138
(617) 868-3900 • fax: (617) 868-2742
Web site: www.nber.org

Founded in 1920, the National Bureau of Economic Research is a private, nonprofit, nonpartisan research organization dedicated to promoting a greater understanding of how the economy works. The NBER is committed to undertaking and disseminating unbiased economic research among public-policy makers, business professionals, and the academic community. NBER publications include, *Body Composition and Wages, The Evolution of Inequality, Heterogeneity and Uncertainty in Labor Earnings in the U.S. Economy,* and *Long-Run Changes in the U.S. Wage Structure: Narrowing, Widening, Polarizing.*

Urban Institute
2100 M St. NW, Washington, DC   20037
(202) 833-7200
Web site: www.urban.org

The Urban Institute analyzes policies, evaluates programs, and informs community development to improve social, civic, and economic well-being. Working in all fifty states and abroad in more than twenty-eight countries, the Urban Institute shares research findings with policy makers, program administrators, businesspersons, academics, and the public online and through reports and scholarly books. Urban Institute publications include, *Increasing the Minimum Wage: Implications and Effects, Low-Wage Workers with Children Face Difficulties Gaining Ground, Low-Income Parents with Work Barriers Are Not Supported by a Comprehensive Service System,* and *Next Steps in Providing Benefits to Low-Wage Workers.*

Bibliography

Books

Francine D. Blau, Marianne A. Ferber, and Anne E. Winkler
The Economics of Women, Men, and Work. Upper Saddle River, NJ: Prentice-Hall, 2006.

Matthew J. DeLuca and Nanette F. DeLuca
Perfect Phrases for Negotiating Salary and Job Offers: Hundreds of Ready-to-Use Phrases to Help You Get the Best Possible Salary, Perks or Promotion. New York: McGraw-Hill, 2006.

Warren Farrell and Karen DeCrow
Why Men Earn More: The Startling Truth Behind the Pay Gap and What Women Can Do About It. New York: AMACOM, 2005.

Robert H. Frank
Falling Behind: How Rising Inequality Harms the Middle Class. Berkeley and Los Angeles: University of California Press, 2007.

Joni Hersch
Sex Discrimination in the Labor Market. Hanover, MA: Now, 2007.

Ira Katznelson
When Affirmative Action Was White: An Untold History of Racial Inequality in Twentieth-Century America. New York: Norton, 2005.

Stephanie Luce
Fighting for a Living Wage. Ithaca, NY: Cornell University Press, 2004.

176

Meizhu Lui, Rebecca Anderson, Betsy Leondar-Wright, Barbara Robles, and Rose Brewer	*Color of Wealth: The Story behind the U.S. Racial Wealth Divide.* New York: New Press, 2006.
Sugata Marjit and Rajat Acharyya	*International Trade, Wage Inequality and the Developing Economy.* New York: Springer-Verlag, 2003.
Deborah Reed and Jennifer Cheng	*Racial and Ethnic Wage Gaps in the California Labor Market.* San Francisco: Public Policy Institute of California, 2003.
Alan Reynolds	*Income and Wealth.* Westport, CT: Greenwood, 2006.
Beth Shulman	*Betrayal of Work: How Low-Wage Jobs Fail 30 Million Americans.* New York: New Press, 2005.
Brian Smedley, Alan Jenkins, and Bill Lan Lee	*All Things Being Equal: Instigating Opportunity in an Inequitable Time.* New York: New Press, 2007.
Barbara Stanny	*Secrets of Six-Figure Women: Surprising Strategies to Up Your Earnings and Change Your Life.* New York: HarperCollins, 2004.
Veronica Jaris Tichenor	*Earning More and Getting Less: Why Successful Wives Can't Buy Equality.* Piscataway, NJ: Rutgers University Press, 2005.

Nancy R. Venneti *Labor, Job Growth, and the Work Place of the Future.* Hauppauge, NY: Nova Science, 2004.

Periodicals

Sigal Alon and Yitchak Haberfeld "Labor Force Attachment and the Evolving Wage Gap Between White, Black, and Hispanic Young Women," *Work and Occupations*, November 2007.

Robert Bartley "'Affirmative Action': Devil in the Details," *Wall Street Journal*, February 10, 2003.

Thomas J. Billitteri "Curbing CEO Pay: Foreigners Resent U.S. CEO's High Pay," *CQ Researcher*, March 9, 2007.

Elaine L. Chao "Knowledge Key to Higher Wages," *Messenger Inquirer* (Kentucky), September 2, 2007.

Ann Crittenden "Don't Get Mad, Get Even," *American Prospect*, May 2006.

Phil Davies "Wives at Work," *Region*, December 2003.

Sandra Davis "Education Holds Key to Improving Wage Gap and Poverty Standards," *Saint John Telegraph-Journal* (New Brunswick, Canada), July 25, 2007.

Maria E. Enchautegui "Immigration and Wage Changes of High School Dropouts," *Monthly Labor Review*, October 1997.

Marilyn Gilory "Hispanic Women Exerting Economic Influence," *Hispanic Outlook
in Higher Education*, February 27,
2006.

Paul Gordon "Central Illinois Nearing Career Crisis—Experts Speak of Urgency in
Training Workforce for Highly Skilled
Jobs;" *Lincoln* (NE) *Journal Star*, October 11, 2007.

John Henry "Arkansas Women Narrow Pay Gap,"
Arkansas Business, November 29,
2004.

Mark A. Hoffman "Employers Score a Win with Pay
Bias Decision; Supreme Court Puts
Firm Limit on Filing Period," *Busi-
ness Insurance*, June 4, 2007.

Chinhui Juhn "Labor Market Dropouts and Trends
in the Wages of Black and White
Men," *Industrial and Labor Relations
Review*, July 1, 2003.

Linda Meric "Wage Gap for Women Narrows—
but Still a Long Way to Go to Parity
with Men!" *Colorado Woman*, April
2003.

Joan Oleck "Poor Literacy Skills Threaten Our
Future: Report Warns that Many
Kids Won't Have a Chance Unless We
Narrow the Achievement Gap," *School
Library Journal*, March 2007.

Deborah Perelman	"Among Tech Execs, Men Face Gender Wage Gap," *eWeek*, January 24, 2007. www.eweek.com.
Garth C. Reeves Jr.	"Blacks Not Seeing the Fruits of Their Labor," *Miami* (FL) *Times*, September 11, 2007.
Robert J. Samuelson	"The Quagmire of Inequality; Citing Income Increases of the Most Wealthy Evokes Images of Greedy CEOs and Hedge-Fund Managers. But the Story Is More Complicated," *Newsweek*, June 11, 2007.
Jennifer Schramm	"Wage Gap Reversals," *HR Magazine*, October 2007.
Keith Sill	"Widening the Wage Gap: The Skill Premium and Technology," *Business Review (Federal Reserve Bank of Philadelphia)*, Winter 2002.
Kelly Weeks, Matthew Weeks, and Lauren Frost	"The Role of Race and Social Class in Compensation Decisions," *Journal of Managerial Psychology*, 2007.

Index